I Prefer to Laugh

One Man, One Family, One Disease

g. d. sullivan

7/29/09
Fred + Barbara
Gary

Edited by

Shawn Patrick Sullivan

I Prefer to Laugh

One Man, One Family, One Disease

Copyright © 2009 Gary Sullivan

Published in the USA by

MadRow

madrow.com

Cover

Artwork by Melissa Kallis Burr

Photo by Jennifer Kearns - Courtesy Goodall Hospital

ISBN 1442122870

EAN-13 9781442122871

Table of Contents

Acknowledgements
Dedication

SECTION I - One Man

SECTION II – One Family

SECTION III – One Disease

ACKNOWLEDGMENTS

My life changed on June 25, 1971. That was the day I became a husband and a man. At that point in my life, I left behind a challenging past and gained control of my future.

I married Lorraine C. Bourre, and she has been my wife and best friend for 38 years. Our family expanded with the birth of our son, Shawn Patrick, on March 28, 1972, and again when our daughter, Kelly Elizabeth, entered the world on June 9, 1975.

It is the foundation of my family that has provided me with a wonderful life. Through the ups and the downs, the laughs and the tears, we have been there for each other. This has never been more apparent than since that fateful day in December 2004, when I was diagnosed with Lou Gehrig's disease.

My brother, John, and sister, JoAnn, and I survived our youth and proved, through the strength of our mother, that we could break the cycle of alcoholism, thereby giving our children brighter futures.

Anita Sullivan Kallis was the warm and gentle matriarch of the Sullivan family. She passed away on November 17, 2008, after suffering a stroke. Ma, we miss you.

i

In addition to my family, I have enjoyed the support of friends, many of whom go back more than 30 years.

I also want to acknowledge a special group, my fellow Spartans from the Class of '64 at St. Ignatius High School. Their love and understanding continues to surround me during these challenging times.

To all my co-workers who ever laughed at my stories, you were the best audience this Irishman could have ever hoped to have.

I want to express my deepest appreciation to my son for editing this book, which, given the content, was often difficult for him. I am also grateful to Diane Sullivan for her assistance in editing the format and for her research.

A special thank you goes to my niece, Melissa Kallis Burr, for the beautiful artwork on the cover and her talented contribution to this undertaking.

As I face the challenges of my illness, I do so with the knowledge that I have led a great life, far exceeding my own personal, professional, and public expectations. As a result, I find myself more accepting of the burden that has been placed on me. I approach the end of my life knowing that I have great memories and no regrets.

Madeline Avonlea Sullivan and Rowen Sullivan Shafer, always remember that Grampy loves you and watches over you.

DEDICATION

In Loving Memory

Carol A. Manning

I had the pleasure of working with Carol Manning for 16 years until I accepted a position in 1996 with the university and she decided to retire. She was a close friend of the family and was a confidant not only to me but also to my wife. I always knew I was in trouble when the two of them would get together or speak on the phone.

Carol was a quadriplegic, the result of a broken neck from a car accident during her senior year at Biddeford High School 50 years ago. She had no feeling from the shoulders down and her fingers were bent as the result of an operation to enable her to hold items, to write, and to type. She was a remarkable individual who decided early on that she would live her life fully and independently.

I lost my dear friend in February 2009. I was honored when her family selected me to give her eulogy. To better understand the unique relationship we shared and to provide some insight into this very special person, I have chosen to share my final words to Carol.

Carol's Eulogy

It is an honor to be asked by Carol's family to give the eulogy for my dear friend because I know how much she loved her family. She spoke often and with great pride about each sister and their respective families. Her nieces and nephews were the joys of her life, and with each generation, the love only grew stronger.

My family was fortunate to be on the receiving end of some of that love. Ours was a relationship that surpassed friendship, and it wasn't until last night that I could find the words to explain how much she meant to Lorraine and me and our two children. For our 25th wedding anniversary, Lorraine and I went to Rome, and it was there at St. Peter's Basilica in the Vatican that we purchased Rosaries for our immediate family. Two white ones for our mothers, two green ones for our children, and one each for Lorraine and me. We bought one more for someone very special to us. Last night, as I knelt by her side, there wrapped around her hands was the seventh Rosary, green with a beautiful gold chain. Carol was that special person.

I first met Carol on August 1, 1980, when I reported for work as the new director of guidance at Biddeford High School. Later, Carol told me that she was more nervous than I was because she didn't know what I might think about a secretary in a wheelchair. I never said a word because the chair was not who she was. I do admit, however, that over the years I never let an opportunity go by when she complained about having a rough day to say, "What do you mean? You've been sitting around all day."

iv

Carol and I worked together for 16 years, but our friendship has lasted more than 28 years.

I can only think of a couple of times when Carol got upset with me.

The first one was when she told me she wanted to celebrate an anniversary. She stated that everyone had an anniversary but her. I said, "What do you want to celebrate?" She replied that it had been 25 years since her accident, and she wanted to have an anniversary. We were all rather shocked, but if that was what she wanted, then that was what we were going to do.

It all went well enough, except for the cake. I had ordered one from Reilly's Bakery and asked them to put "Happy 25th Anniversary, George and Mary" on the top. Carol asked why their name was on her cake. I replied that George and Mary had a big fight and cancelled their party, so I got the cake at a discount.

She was very upset – not because she didn't like the cake, but because she thought that I did not care enough to pay full price.

The other time was when our office received a package that had a wide strip of bubble wrap in it. In order for Carol to get to the front desk, the restroom, or the copier, she had to go through the narrow hallway just outside my office door. I covered the floor in that hallway with the bubble wrap, so that every time she went by in her wheelchair it sounded like the Fourth of July. She asked me to remove the bubble wrap, but I wouldn't; I had been laughing too hard, which didn't help the situation.

Now that she has gone before me, I am really concerned that she has lined the entrance to the Pearly Gates with bubble wrap in anticipation of my arrival.

Carol, we thank you for your smile, for your love, and for teaching us all how to deal with life's challenges.

You are greatly missed, my dear friend.

SECTION I

ONE MAN

CHAPTER 1

"I CAN'T GET UP"

The drug, Rilutek; the time, 10:48 p.m. It was my first personal act of acknowledging I had Amyotrophic Lateral Sclerosis (ALS.)

Two days earlier, my neurologist said he was absolutely certain that I had Lou Gehrig's disease. It was 15 days before Christmas.

Rilutek's brand name is Riluzule and it is currently the only medication available to treat ALS, known as Lou Gehrig's disease. I take it orally twice a day.

I had spent 48 hours telling my siblings I had ALS, soft-peddling the news to my 82-year-old mother, and informing my co-workers, my in-laws, and my best friends.

Forty-eight hours of talking about it, but at 10:48 p.m. on December 10, 2004, as I took my first dose of Rilutek, I realized that I had ALS.

Rilutek's pharmaceutical description is careful to note that it is "not a cure for ALS, but has shown to slow progression of the disease." The time gained is measured in months, not years.

Throughout my life, I've had defining moments that have altered the path I've traveled. That initial dose of Rilutek was one of those moments.

This is where the end of my story begins.

* * *

On December 8, 2004, Lou Gehrig's disease took away my future. My life, as I had known it for 59 years, had ended.

"How certain are you?" my wife asked my neurologist.

"One-hundred percent certain," he replied.

His words cut through my heart and pierced my soul.

In an instant, my golden years vanished. Never again would I view dreams with anticipation, or retirement with excitement. The dreams became nightmares; retirement, a disability.

For the next eight weeks, each day began with fear and ended in sadness. When I went to bed, I wasn't afraid I'd not wake up; instead, I was terrified I would. I do not dread death; I dread dying. As this cruel disease progresses, my body will become paralyzed, muscle by muscle, but my mind — my thoughts, my memories, my personality — will remain intact.

Losing independence will strip me of my dignity, my self-esteem, my pride.

"We're all dying," well-meaning friends remind me. "I could drop dead tomorrow," others add. They mean well, but no words can console me. There is no greater isolation than knowing your demise is imminent.

I welcome death. I crave its finality.

* * *

On the Saturday before I was diagnosed, my wife, Lorraine, and I went to Boston to see The Rockettes perform their Radio City Christmas Show at the Wang Center. We enjoyed the program; the dancers radiated with holiday spirit, amid the elegant Christmas décor of the opera house.

During the intermission, I bought a bottle of water at a price that makes a barrel of oil seem cheap. When the show was over I put on my coat and carefully placed the bottle of this precious commodity in my pocket.

As Lorraine and I left the Wang Center, we figured we had just enough time to make the 4:15 Mass at St. Anthony's Chapel across town. We liked the idea of catching Mass in Boston and sleeping in the next morning at home.

The walk to church proved a hike and took longer than we anticipated. My lower legs gave me trouble while I walked, and I was exhausted by the time we arrived at St. Anthony's. We were late too; the priest was well into the service.

We entered the church on the left-hand side and headed down the aisle. We stopped at a pew that was to our right. Then, as I had done throughout my life, I dropped to my right knee to genuflect only this time was different.

3

"I can't get up," I whispered to my wife out of the corner of my mouth.

"What?" she replied.

"I can't get up."

I placed my palms on the chapel's cold stone floor and tried to hoist myself up. I heard a loud thump.

My bottle of water had tumbled from my coat pocket and rolled down the aisle.

Later, my kids, Shawn and Kelly, asked me how I managed to stand back up. I told them I had no idea. I had been so mortified by the spectacle that the next thing I knew I was on my feet, water bottle in hand.

I had genuflected, and I couldn't get up!

Five days later, in my neurologist's office, I'd be brought to my knees once again.

In some ways, the incident at St. Anthony's Church should not have surprised me. Eight months earlier, in April of 2004, I rushed into a local supermarket in my hometown of Sanford, Maine. As I turned into the frozen-food aisle, my right foot had dropped, and I stubbed it on the floor. I flew across the aisle and landed in the arms of a man clutching his groceries.

Desperate for balance, I clung to him, with my arms locked around his neck. As I slid down his body, I heard potato chips crumbling between us.

4

Embarrassed, I apologized profusely. He smiled and replied graciously that he was just glad he was there to catch me.

When I attended Catholic school in the 1960s, close body contact like that would have meant the guy in the frozen food section and I were going steady. The Ursuline Sisters at St. Ignatius would not have tolerated that. Expulsion would have been the least of our problems.

But this wasn't the 60s. Instead, I was nearing 60, and something was wrong with my balance.

My right foot had dropped, causing me to fall, and I didn't know why.

But then balance has never been my strong suit. In the mid-1980s, Lorraine and I went shopping at Jordan Marsh in New Hampshire. I grabbed a pair of pants off the rack and headed to a stall in the fitting room to try them on.

I hate trying on clothes, so I decided to skip the hassle of taking off my shoes. I dropped my pants down to my ankles and started to wrangle out of them by standing on one foot and sliding the pant leg over my shoe on the other foot.

I began to lose my balance. Quickly, I leaned against the wall of the stall to stop myself from falling.

The problem was, it wasn't a wall.

The stall's door flew open, and I lurched into the aisle on one foot, a middle-aged man with pale bowed legs, hopping around in his underwear in full view of the entire men's department of Jordan Marsh. I hobbled back into the stall as quickly as I could and slammed the door. Nobody in the store asked for an encore.

After the incident in the supermarket, I searched the Internet to find a condition that matched my symptoms. I didn't like what I found.

I called my wife into the room to look at the screen. We both fell silent.

The computer was indicating that my symptoms were associated with Lou Gehrig's disease.

***

A couple of weeks later, my primary care physician referred me to a neurologist in Maine. I needed one to examine a pinched nerve in my neck that was causing pain to shoot down my right arm into my hand. I was losing control of my right thumb.

As my neurologist checked my arm, I told him about my right foot. He performed an Electromyography (EMG), which tests the electrical activity of muscles. He stuck pins into me that sent electric signals through my limbs. The EMG's results indicated that there was nothing specifically wrong with my foot, but that a pinched nerve in my back or behind my right knee might have been causing it to drop.

My neurologist told me his remedy: "Don't cross your legs."

Simple enough. Throughout my life I had crossed my legs

while sitting. According to my neurologist, all I had to do was stop, and my right foot would return to normal.

Needless to say, Lorraine and I were relieved. I didn't have ALS. I vowed never again to use the Internet to diagnose my ailments.

That summer, I had another appointment with my primary care physician. I asked him if the pain in my arm, the atrophy of my thumb, and the problem with my right foot were simply things with which I'd have to live.

"No," he emphasized, and scheduled me for two more appointments. The first would be with my neurologist again, the second with a neurosurgeon in Maine.

I met with my neurologist in July and again in September, and each time I questioned him about my foot. He asked me to walk down the hall and back, just outside his office, which I did. He watched me but did not indicate anything serious when I finished. He concurred, though, that I needed to see a neurosurgeon about the pinched nerve in my neck and its effect on my right arm and hand.

At the end of September, I saw the surgeon, who examined me and discovered bone spurs between two upper discs on my spine. He recommended surgery to fix the problem and to avoid a "further neurological downturn," as he put it in his notes.

On October 14, 2004, I reported to Mercy Hospital in Portland, Maine, for surgery. The procedure took part of the morning, and I was home by the afternoon. I took the next few days off from work, sleeping in, taking walks down Main

Street, and just taking it easy.

It *sounds* relaxing, but that's not an easy assignment for a Type-A personality like me. One day, my son drove down Main Street and pulled over when he saw me standing before a storefront window.

"I knew you'd be bored with nothing to do all day, but I didn't think it would come to this," he said as he rolled down his car window.

I laughed. I had been staring at a display of stuffed animals.

The good news was that my right arm, hand, and thumb had immediately begun to improve. Unfortunately, my right foot had not, but that was not unexpected. The general medical consensus was that my problems with my arm and foot were unrelated. My neurologist saw no need for me to make any more appointments.

I met with my surgeon again at the end of November as a follow-up to my surgery. I mentioned to him the problem I kept having with my right foot dropping. I also told him that my left foot was starting to have the same problem and that both of my ankles had been stripped to skin and bones with no sign of muscle.

He asked to see my ankles. He didn't hesitate when he saw them; he immediately told me I needed to go back to the neurologist.

My surgeon wrote a note to my neurologist, providing him with my recent medical history and noting the increased atrophy in both of my legs. He recommended another test of my lower extremities, and he concluded by noting "it is conceivable that we have been misled by the more common statin-related problems."

By "common statin-related problems," my surgeon was referring to the weakness in my legs that I had experienced while taking the drug Lipitor to control my cholesterol. I started taking Lipitor in 1999; in the years that followed, I lost strength and energy in both legs, particularly whenever I walked up hills. I stopped taking Lipitor in the fall of 2003; as a result, I started experiencing fewer muscle cramps and better strength in my legs. By March 2004, I felt better than I had in years. A month later, I began to have problems with my right foot.

Before I left my surgeon's office, I informed his nurse that I did not want to return to the same neurologist and preferred to make an appointment with his partner. That summer, I had become frustrated, even offended, by the blatant lack of professionalism of my neurologist and his staff.

His office failed to make sure my medical records had been transferred to my surgeon. When I inquired about it, I was told that I should pick up my records at their office and bring them to the appointment myself — an inconvenience made all the more frustrating by the fact that my neurologist's office is directly above my surgeon's.

Once I picked up my records, I took a moment to go back to my car to look them over. I made an appalling discovery — instead of my test results, my neurologist's office had given me those of another patient.

I returned the other patient's test results to the receptionist and asked for my own. She disappeared for a moment, and then returned and informed me that the employee who handles those records was "out to lunch." She said she'd send my records down to my surgeon's office once her co-worker returned. They did not arrive in time for my appointment.

At my request, an appointment was scheduled with a different neurologist on Wednesday, December 8. On the Friday before, I received a call asking me to report to the neurologist for some tests on Monday, December 6. I figured the new doctor wanted me to be tested that Monday, so that he could have the results to discuss with me two days later.

I reported to the office on Monday, only to learn I'd be seeing my old neurologist, not his partner. I told the receptionist that I had reasons for not wanting to deal with same neurologist.

Timing did me no favors. At that moment, my old neurologist walked into the waiting room and called out my name. Not knowing what to do, I decided to go with him. Within minutes, I'd deeply regret it.

After he ran a few brief tests, he took a seat and said, "It's not muscular; it's neurological."

"I know what 'muscular' is, but what's neurological?" I replied.

Without emotion or compassion, my neurologist spoke and changed my life forever.

"It's Lou Gehrig's disease."

10

* * *

I had always been under the impression that ALS was a muscular disease. I found out the hard way I was wrong.

The neurologist told me he wanted me to have another MRI, as well as have some blood drawn before he made his diagnosis definite. He told me to come back on Wednesday. He said nothing more.

I went to the doctor's office alone that Monday because I believed I'd be going in for a test. I never thought I'd be diagnosed, let alone so quickly and coldly. My neurologist had just thrust back into my life what I had feared eight months earlier, when Lorraine and I saw "ALS" on our computer screen.

This had nothing to do with crossing my legs. How could the computer have been so right and my neurologist so wrong?

According to my medical records, my neurologist wrote back to my surgeon after my appointment that Monday.

"Mr. Sullivan has shown progressive weakness, now involving both lower extremities since last seen in the summer," he wrote, attributing the condition to motor nerve loss. "A diagnosis of a motor neuron disease seems most likely."

Stunned, I walked out of the doctor's office desperate to cling to any sanity I had left. Before my appointment — a lifetime ago, when I calmly and safely assumed I'd only be going in for tests — I had planned to go to Arby's afterward for a quick lunch. I decided to stick with that decision.

I pulled into the restaurant's parking lot and found I couldn't get out of my car. The tears I'd held back moments earlier now ran down my cheeks. I wept uncontrollably.

Aching for that comfort food, I resolved to order at the drive-thru. Since I could not stop crying, I turned away from the loudspeaker, faced the passenger's seat, and shouted my order, all in an effort to avoid being seen crying. Thinking back on it, I'm sure I looked more ridiculous than if I had simply faced the right way and ordered as I wept.

I took my food and drove to Portland's Eastern Promenade, overlooking Casco Bay. I've known this place since I was a child. My uncle served as the park's supervisor and lived in a house that faced the ocean, a perk afforded him by his position. I often visited his family. We'd sit on the back lawn and drink iced tea — always bitter, never sweetened, without lemons, freshly brewed.

Over the years, I'd return to the Promenade, sometimes to "park" with my girlfriend, now my wife, or eat an Italian sandwich from Amato's, the home of the original, on India Street. Later, Lorraine and I would bring our kids and our collie, Shannon, to run in the grass and play in the park.

I had not been to the Promenade in years. When I returned there that Monday in December, I parked beneath the bandstand overlooking the bay. Everything was different. Instead of eating an Amato's Italian, I chewed slowly on a roast-beef sandwich from Arby's. In place of the good times, a nightmare had begun.

I ate my lunch and then called Lorraine. I simply asked her if she could leave work and meet me at home. I told her I'd be there in 45 minutes.

She asked me how my appointment went, and I replied, "Not well."

That's all we said. Lorraine knew things were bad, but she couldn't have imagined the magnitude. Our life, as we had enjoyed it for more than 33 years, would never be the same.

Less than an hour later, we both stood in our kitchen, and I uttered the words I had been told hours earlier.

"Lou Gehrig's disease."

We hugged, and we cried.

Lorraine called our two grown children, Shawn and Kelly, to inform them we were driving down to see them. At the time, they both were living in the same community in New Hampshire. We agreed we'd all meet at Kelly's place within the hour.

When we gathered, I told my son and daughter the news. We hugged, and we cried.

There'd be a lot of crying in the weeks and months ahead.

Two days later, on Wednesday, December 8, I returned to my neurologist's office. This time Lorraine accompanied me.

He confirmed his diagnosis, with "one-hundred percent certainty." My MRI from the day before showed nothing unusual, and the results of my blood test were not yet available.

I found it ironic that the doctor who saw nothing wrong with me for nine months now didn't need to see my blood results before he confirmed I had a disease known for being difficult to diagnose.

When we left the doctor's office I told Lorraine that I wanted to go grab a bite to eat at Tim Horton's.

"Are you sure?" she asked.

"Yes," I replied. "I want to do normal."

At Tim Horton's we sat, and we ate. We didn't hug, and we didn't cry. We did "normal," for 45 minutes, at least.

Then I called my brother, John; our family calls him "Butch." I told him to track down our sister, JoAnn, and ask her to meet both of us at his house. I didn't give him a reason, and he didn't ask for one. He knew it couldn't be good, but he couldn't have comprehended how bad it would be.

Lorraine and I arrived at Butch's house an hour later. JoAnn was not there yet, but we proceeded to tell Butch and his wife, Terry, the news: "I have Lou Gehrig's disease."

They were devastated.

My sister arrived moments later. When I told her, she hugged me, and as we embraced, she began to beat her fists against my back.

"No, no, you can't have that!" she cried.

It didn't make sense to her that her kid brother, the

youngest in the family, could be so fatally sick.

* * *

My wife, brother, and sister are private people, but I'm more open about my life. In the days following my diagnosis, I organized my thoughts and decided how and when I'd make my situation public. I first told my wife I had ALS, and then we told our children. Then I told my brother and sister. Now, I had to tell my mother.

My mother, Anita, was a wonderful woman, who encouraged and ensured the successes my brother, sister, and I have achieved throughout our lives.

We have tremendous respect for this lovely lady, who had known tragedy not once, but twice, when she lost two husbands, one to alcoholism, the other to Alzheimer's disease.

I was always the one to make Mom laugh. For example, one time, I caught her with her foot in her mouth, and I chided her about it for years.

My son and his wife, Valerie, told my mother they were expecting their first child. My mom expressed great joy, and leaned forward and offered them some advice.

"Two is a good number of children to have," she told them.

I was right beside her at the time.

"Ma, I'm your third child," I said.

"Yes, I know," she replied, not quite realizing that she had implied she should have quit after Butch and JoAnn.

I used to remind my mother about her remark whenever the opportunity arose. I would always feign great woundedness for good measure.

"I'm never going to live that down, am I?" she asked and laughed.

"No, Ma," I told her, "you never will."

How was I to tell my own mother that her youngest child was dying?

Butch, Jo-Ann, and I talked it over, and we decided that my brother and I would go see Mom together and tell her about my diagnosis. We decided we'd refer to the disease as "ALS," rather than "Lou Gehrig's disease," because she and others of her generation tend not to know the illness by its initials. Butch and I told Mom the news, but we sugarcoated it in an effort to protect her, and that soon proved a mistake.

Days later, I visited Mom and told her, "I've noticed you haven't asked me any questions about my illness. Do you have any? I will answer anything you ask."

She paused and said, "My neighbor told me that ALS is Lou Gehrig's disease. But it isn't, is it?"

My heart broke.

"Yeah, it is, Ma," I said.

16

Mom tried not to cry in front of me. I told her I felt fine, that the disease was progressing slowly. It didn't matter. It broke my heart because I knew it shattered hers.

She told me that she suspected the news had to be worse than Butch and I originally let on. She said she knew because the last time my brother and I both went to break news to her, eleven years earlier, it was to tell her JoAnn had a brain tumor and needed an operation.

"I am concerned that you aren't telling me everything," she said.

"I will promise to tell you everything," I responded. "But you need to promise not to worry if I do."

"OK," she answered.

I knew it was a promise that she could not keep. She never showed me how worried she was, and I guess that was her way of keeping her word.

I made one more promise to her, that I would not die before her. I could not let her face the agony of losing a child.

I had gone out on a limb because she was healthy and independent at the time, and my life expectancy was two to five years.

My mother suffered a stroke in the fall of 2008. She died on November 17, 2008, at the age of 86.

Lorraine and I were the only family not by her bedside that evening. We were in Connecticut when we learned Ma had taken a turn for the worse, and we were rushing home when she passed. I think she wanted it that way. I would not die before her, and she did not want to die in front of me.

Upon arriving at the nursing home, we rushed to her room, and my family let me sit by her side in private.

"I kept my promise, Ma," I told her.

***

I have been open with others about my illness since Day One. My wife, a shy and private person, would have kept it quiet had she been the one who was sick; only immediate family would know. I'm different.

My personal physician asked me why I told people about my ALS before I got my second opinion at Massachusetts General Hospital (MGH) in January 2005. He told me he would have waited. Not me. I'm different.

My neurologist said he was "one-hundred percent certain" I had ALS. I'm a realist.

My approach has sometimes made it difficult for others. After my diagnosis, I kept working as the Director of the University College and visiting friends and letting them know my situation.

At one point, Lorraine cautioned me not to overexert myself.

"I'm not sick," I snapped, "I'm *dying*."

My retort made perfect sense to me, but it hurt my wife. I felt badly.

As a realist, though, I knew what I meant. My ALS was in its earliest stages, and I still felt well. I was not in any pain, and I barely felt any discomfort. I did not see myself as ill; instead, I had a disease that would take my life some other day, but not that day.

I was not ill. I was simply dying.

I notice the impact on others when I tell them I have ALS. Anguish overtakes their faces. It's in their eyes. It's in their words of sympathy and comfort. It's in the way they ask if there's anything they can do to help, even though they know there's little they can do because ALS has no cure.

It's like being at my own wake.

The love and support I experienced in the months after my diagnosis overwhelmed me and nursed my shattered spirit.

I Prefer to Laugh

CHAPTER 2

DEFINING MOMENTS

My favorite poet, Robert Frost, wrote in the last verse of his poem, "The Road Not Taken:"

> *I shall be telling this with a sigh*
> *Somewhere ages and ages hence:*
> *Two roads diverged in a wood, and I -*
> *I took the one less traveled by,*
> *And that has made all the difference.*

This verse brings to mind a conversation I had as a guidance director with three of my colleagues at Biddeford High School. We were trying to outdo one another on the economic status of our childhoods.

"I was so poor that I had a used bike," one counselor stated.

"I was so poor that I had to make a bike from used parts," the second counselor chimed in.

21

Not to be outdone, the principal responded, "I was so poor I had to make a bike from stolen parts."

"You guys had bikes?" I replied.

Our lives are often defined by the decisions we make. For the four of us, it was education that was the "road less traveled by" that proved to be a defining moment. It provided each of us with a better quality of life through which to peddle a new bicycle.

Then there are those defining moments not of our making, events so powerful that they alter the road upon which we will travel.

As a child, living in a home ravaged by my father's alcoholism, it was not a straight path on which I journeyed but one of many curves and unexpected obstacles.

In alcoholic families, there is a child whose "job" it is to maintain the peace by being "good." That was my role.

I lived in constant fear that my behavior would trigger my father's drinking. Even when he was sober, the threat of setting him off persisted. Eventually, I came to realize that he and he alone was responsible for his behavior.

That conclusion proved important when I was 22 and a junior at the University of Maine at Orono.

It was homecoming weekend and my friends and I were preparing for the festivities when someone informed me that I had a visitor. It was my brother-in-law, Alan. At first I was excited and even asked if he and my sister had come up for homecoming. Then I realized that neither of them had attended the University of Maine and, therefore, had no reason to participate in alumni activities.

Alan didn't have to tell me. I knew. *It's my Dad,* I thought. My brother-in-law confirmed my suspicions. I responded with three simple words: "He killed himself." It was not a question but an acknowledgement of what I had known would only be a matter of time.

Throughout my childhood, my father repeatedly enacted suicide attempts. Deep down, I knew that some day he would realize he could no longer tolerate who he had become.

My Dad was an intelligent individual. He had great leadership skills demonstrated by the variety of positions he held. He had been president of a union, the Little League, and my school's boosters club. What he didn't have was personal fortitude. He made several attempts at sobriety but with no success.

Growing up, I rarely spoke about my Dad's drinking, but I do recall one time when a friend picked me up to go for a ride. When I got in the car, I stated, "My father won't be here when I return."

That night, Dad had tried another of his faux suicide attempts. He barely cut himself as he lay in the upstairs bedroom with a knife on the floor. That was his *modus operandi* — attempts that didn't warrant medical attention. Instead, it was the attention he sought as he waited for one of us to discover him.

I knew Dad wouldn't be home that night because my family had called the sheriff to pick him up and escort him to the

23

hospital in Augusta.

In the sixties there were no treatment centers for alcoholics, no rehab facilities, no programs to which he or our family could turn. The concept of intervention had not yet been introduced. There were only institutions where alcoholics shared space with the mentally ill.

It was Dad's third time in Augusta. He chose to go the first two times, in failed attempts to defeat the demons he had inherited from his father.

This time my family and I had him admitted because we no longer knew how to protect him from himself.

A couple of weeks later, my mother, brother, sister, and I traveled 90 miles to Augusta to visit my Dad. As he shared with us the horrors of living with the mentally ill, we knew we could not leave him there. He came home, never to return there as his alcoholism began to spin out of control.

Therefore, I was not surprised on that warm sunny Friday in October. I brought my brother-in-law to my room as I made preparations for my trip home to bury the father I loved.

My head was clear. I needed to pack my suit and plenty of handkerchiefs.

Alan and I joined my sister, who had waited in the car. In those days, women were not allowed in men's dorms and vice versa.

Orono is three hours north of Sanford, and it was a somber trip. When we arrived home in the early evening, the house was filled with our extended family who had gathered to support us.

Upon returning home following my Dad's burial, I went up to my bedroom and broke down. My Uncle Eddie, Dad's only brother, came into the room. I shared with him what scared me the most. I was so similar to my Dad in personality, leadership, and the Irish wit. Would I become my father's son?

It wasn't until 35 years later that I realized the full impact my father's death had on me.

I was at the top of my career as Director of the University Colleges at Saco and Sanford, a division of the University of Maine System. I was respected in the community, I had been appointed to the board of trustees of the hospital, and I was blessed with a strong and close family.

I was completely surprised when, in 2002, I suffered severe panic attacks during a two-week period. I sought counseling. During this time, I woke up at six one Saturday morning, which is something I never do on the weekend. I went downstairs and sat at the dining room table. Lorraine, a morning person, was already up; she asked if I was OK. Out of nowhere, I blurted, "I tried to be perfect, and the son of a bitch killed himself anyway."

The anxiety attacks stopped.

Nearly four decades after his death, the ghost of my father left my body.

* * *

Now I'm facing the most challenging, defining moment of my life. I am traveling down a different road, one with many potholes and hazards, into the unknown world of Amyotrophic Lateral Sclerosis.

Six weeks after my diagnosis, I realized what this illness had done to me. It had broken my spirit. My spirit is a combination of my personality, character, and love of life — my very being.

There have been times when my spirit has been severely bruised — my Dad's suicide; my step-dad's Alzheimer's disease; my sister's brain tumor — but it had always withstood the beating and remained intact. Now it was broken and only time, a sparse commodity for me, would tell if it would ever return.

There are times when I forget I'm dying. A good laugh with a friend, a rare television show or movie, or a special moment with my grandchildren will fill my mind with something other than ALS. However, the predominant thought, the overpowering thought, the thought of one's own personal demise, is so all encompassing that it gives the mind little rest.

Since my diagnosis I have endured an array of emotions. One of them was the shock of the diagnosis itself.

I often think back over those early days and wonder how I survived.

How did I get up from that chair and walk out of the neurologist's office?

How did I stop and order lunch before calling my wife?

How did I make it through the eight weeks that followed?

That day altered my way of thinking, of viewing the world around me, and the way people view me.

During that first year, I had no way of knowing whether my ALS was progressing quickly or slowly. I didn't know if in six months I'd be walking or even talking. No one had a crystal ball that had the answers.

Gradually, it became clear that the pace of my ALS seemed to be slow. But how slow?

Lou Gehrig's disease is like the snow that falls in midwinter in New England. It can come as a blizzard or as a light snowfall, in which you can almost make out the uniqueness of each flake. In both cases, it's the accumulation that can shut down the hardiest of souls.

In the blizzard, the pace is quick and the resulting paralysis is sudden. With a drawn-out shower, the ultimate accumulation may be the same, only it takes longer to get there.

I've seen individuals whose ALS has come in like a blizzard. Mine is more like a slow, endless snow shower, with the accumulation slowly but steadily increasing.

One day, I crossed paths with a gentleman I respect. "How are you feeling?" I asked him.

He had had an operation and I was concerned. I guess I pressed a little too hard, for his response was, "I am doing fine, and if I wasn't, I wouldn't tell anyone, anyway."

He is a private person; I am not. I respected his sentiments and have taken note since. I am not sure whether his retort was intended to carry a message — it did.

I realize not everyone agrees with, or even understands, my openness regarding my disease. To remain quiet would not be me. At some point my gait, my brace, and my fatigue would become obvious, leading to speculation and rumors.

During the day, I deal with my Lou Gehrig's disease academically. That is my training, my experience, and my personality.

While ALS is academic for me during the day, it becomes personal at night. It is overwhelming.

How I miss the daily routine of work, the challenges it posed, and the interaction it required.

How I dread the loneliness that exists even when I am with people.

I have an illness that will eventually leave me powerless, motionless, speechless.

I desperately want to be that person that everyone remembers and not the individual I have become.

Because my ALS is slow and I can hide many of its effects, I sometimes wonder if I'm doing a disservice to those who have a more progressive form of this illness.

I even feel guilty when I hear of people with ALS (pALS) who were diagnosed after me and are now restricted to a wheelchair, or are on a ventilator, unable to communicate, or even to move.

I have chosen to do what I can for as long as I can to attack this horrific illness. I owe it to pALS who cannot.

The pace of my illness is a mixed bag. My son once asked me an interesting question.

"Dad, is the fact that your ALS is moving so slowly good news because you have more time to do things and longer to live? Or is it like water torture, where it is a slow, tormenting drip-by-drip process?"

His question struck me. I found it insightful, and no one had ever asked it before.

"It's a little of both," I replied.

I'm pleased that I get to spend more time with my loved ones. I get to continue to do some of the things I enjoy. Nevertheless, the slow ticking of time is a heavy burden. I know my disease. I'm aware of its stages, and its ultimate outcome is so horrific and unimaginable that living with that knowledge makes the slow progression as much a curse as a blessing.

I Prefer to Laugh

CHAPTER 3

"I'M SORRY, SO SORRY..."

One summer day, several years back, I was home alone. The weather was warm, a slight breeze was blowing, and all the windows were open. The family was out of the house, so I seized the moment and burst into song. I'm a terrible singer; I don't often get the opportunity to sing. The only two songs I know are "Happy Birthday" and the national anthem. Both are usually sung by large enough groups of people to drown out my voice.

So there I was, belting out at the top of my lungs my rendition of the United States' most revered song.

"Oh, say, can you see, by the dawn's early light,
what so proudly we hail'd at the twilight's last
gleaming?...."

Two weeks passed. As I sat in my back yard, my neighbor, Glenna, an older woman whose second-floor porch faces our back yard, yelled out, *"I have a bone to pick with you!"*

31

I was taken aback because we had always gotten along.

Concerned, I replied, "Why? What did I do?"

Glenna answered that a few weeks earlier she had heard me singing and had laughed so hard she hurt her stomach muscles and ended up at the hospital. She was just then recovering from the terrible pain my singing had inflicted upon her.

I am now required by town ordinance to give neighbors fair warning should the mood to sing ever strike me again.

I've frequently felt reflective and nostalgic since my diagnosis. One particular morning, I found myself singing an old tune from my youth while in the shower − not a pretty scene, visually or musically, but it remains the only place where I am allowed to sing.

I was singing an old Brenda Lee song, and it included the words, "I'm sorry, so sorry, please accept my apology."

In the days after my diagnosis, I found myself not singing but apologizing.

I would say I'm sorry to my wife for what was happening to us and to our future and to my children for taking away the happiness of new jobs, new homes, and for the sadness this illness has brought to my family.

"I'm sorry, so sorry, please accept my apology."

One night our cat, O'Rourke, came up to me in bed. As I petted him, I cried and apologized to him for not giving him more attention.

I love O'Rourke, but I knew I'd gone too far when I apologized to him. He's a cat; he doesn't understand. I stopped apologizing for something over which I had no control.

I stopped, that is, until Mother's Day 2005. I had not gotten my wife a gift, which was unlike me. No card, no gift, could say what I felt.

I found Lorraine in our study, and we embraced. Once again, I uttered the words, "I'm sorry, so sorry."

I was sorry for all the pain this disease would cause. Sorry that it has destroyed our future and for what she was about to go through as my caregiver.

Someone who cares for a person with a terminal illness faces difficult challenges — even more so when the person has ALS.

I don't view a spouse as a "caregiver." For two individuals, who have spent the majority of their lives together, it's not "caregiving," but a labor of love. It's the truest test of the wedding vows, "in sickness and in health."

I had no doubt that Lorraine would be at my side throughout the balance of my life as I would be for her.

Lorraine is a strong individual with deep love and religious convictions. While she is not a public person, I am confident that my wife has the strength to deal with the challenges that lie before us.

***

My wife claims to be an introvert but I know her dark secret and checkered past. I can no longer enable her actions. Her story must be told. My wife is a secret "celebrity stalker."

I was too close to recognize Lorraine's symptoms: her racing heartbeat; her heightened excitement; and her complete loss of inhibitions.

In 1975, we reserved a room at the Holiday Inn by the Bay in Portland and purchased two tickets to see Bob Hope at the Cumberland County Civic Center. After the show, we returned to the hotel and took the elevator to our floor. As we got out of the elevator, Lorraine turned to me and said, "Did you notice who that was?"

"Who?"

"The man on the elevator," she stated. "He was Hope's guitarist, and he pressed 11."

That's when the nightmare began.

"I'm going to see Bob Hope!" Lorraine announced. "Are you coming?"

"No," I replied, shocked. "There's no way you'll find him."

It was all downhill from there. Lorraine left and took the elevator to the 11th floor. She proceeded down the corridor, going from side to side and door to door, listening for Bob Hope's voice.

She found two couples knocking on a door. Bob Hope answered. Recognizing them as old friends, he invited them in. And who should follow them but my wife, the self-proclaimed introvert?

Hope ignored her as he and his friends exchanged pleasantries about his wife, Delores, and their good friend, Mamie Eisenhower.

Finally, one of the women turned to my wife and said, "This young woman happened to be walking by when we came in."

At that point, Hope acknowledged Lorraine and shook her hand and gave her his autograph.

Years later, we returned to the Civic Center to see Liza Minnelli in concert. After the show, Lorraine insisted on waiting near the exit, where she had spotted a limousine. She quickly staked out her position. I kept a good 20 feet away. Minnelli appeared and started getting into her car. That's when my "introverted" wife reached over the car door and grabbed Minnelli's shoulder. I was horrified, as was Minnelli's security detail.

Then there was the time, in 1990, when my son got us back-stage passes to see Jay Leno after his performance at the Merrill Auditorium in Portland. As we proceeded backstage, I once again saw the telltale signs on my wife: glazed-over eyes;

intensified focus; and the stance of a woman on a mission. As Leno reached out to shake Lorraine's hand, she asked him for a kiss, to which he replied, "To hell with that — let's go in the back room."

It doesn't stop there.

In 1995, we went to a show at the South Shore Music Circus in Cohasset, Massachusetts, and we had reserved rooms at Kimball's By-the-Sea. Spotting a limo outside the front door, Lorraine stationed herself by the elevator and acted completely surprised when Regis Philbin, star of that night's show, stepped off the elevator. My wife shook his hand.

Returning to Kimball's after Regis's performance, we went to the hotel's lounge for a nightcap. After 10 minutes in a large room with great hors d'oeuvres, we were asked to leave what turned out to be a private party for "Reege."

Still in search of a good Margarita on the rocks, we went to an outside patio, where we sat alone, overlooking the water. Alone, that is, until Suzanne Somers, Regis's co-star for that evening, arrived with her husband and another couple. And there it was: the glaze, the determination, and the no-holding-her-back stance. Lorraine approached Somers and thanked her for a lovely performance. Me? I was just thankful she didn't grab the star's shoulder.

Once, on a trip to Vermont, Lorraine was determined to find Michael J. Fox's home, which he had purchased near Woodstock. Even though the townspeople were sworn to secrecy, they were no match for my wife, the "introvert."

As we approached Fox's brick farmhouse, Lorraine got out of our car and ran to the house, right past the "Do Not Trespass" sign, and looked in Fox's window.

To this day, I thank my lucky stars that Fox was not at home.

You can imagine my trepidation as my wife and I decided to celebrate our 30th anniversary in New York City, Mecca to the stars. As we were returning to our hotel after an excellent performance of the "Lion King," Lorraine's eyes began to glaze over, her heart began to race, and I recognized that determined stare. I knew there would be trouble. There, in front of the St. James Theater, were two Town cars, a small crowd, and the telltale sign of a star sighting: barricades.

The stars of New York's hottest show, "The Producers," were my wife's next conquest as she positioned herself for a close-up view of Nathan Lane and Matthew Broderick. She got Broderick's autograph, for he was no match for "The Introvert."

The next day, while we were having lunch at Carnegie's Deli, sandwich-maker to the stars, we were seated next to two gentlemen. As I took a bite out of my six-inch-high pastrami sandwich, my eyes met my wife's — they had that look. I could tell her heart was pounding, and I felt the determination. I gave her a look that said, "Don't you dare."

She ignored me.

With resignation, I whispered, "Well, at least wait until I get up to pay the check."

I was barely out of my seat when she leaned over to one of our tablemates and asked, "Are you who I think you are?"

He wasn't, or so he said.

***

It is that very spirit, zest for life, and determination that Lorraine now draws upon as we battle my Lou Gehrig's disease.

Throughout our 38 years together, she has been unwavering in her faith and in her dedication and commitment to our family.

Within two years of my diagnosis, Lorraine lost her sister, her mother, and her brother-in-law.

It is with amazing strength and courage that she confronts adversity, and she is once again drawing upon it as my ALS progresses in a downward spiral.

This was evident on Sunday, September 17, 2006, when she was called upon to demonstrate that strength.

While eating a hamburger at one of our favorite places in Dover, New Hampshire, I began to gasp for air. I made no sounds, indicating that no air was passing through my windpipe.

I got up to leave the restaurant to spare myself from further embarrassment. Lorraine pointed to the cashier and shouted, *"Call 911!"*

She jerked me around and clutched her arms around me. She locked her hands under my chest and performed the Heimlich Maneuver.

I felt a large glob of food shoot up my throat and fill my mouth.

I grasped for air. This time there was noise. The blockage had been cleared.

It had happened. Less than two weeks after my speech pathologist at MGH urged us to learn the Heimlich Maneuver, my wife was called upon to use it, even without the training.

Once outside the restaurant, I sat on a bench and continued to gasp for air. My breathing slowly returned to normal.

I had reached a new phase, one that brought death that much closer. While I had not been at death's door, I was on its stone walkway.

I asked Lorraine to cancel the 911 call and to get my soda and some napkins because I still had the food in my mouth. I didn't want to spit it out because that would have worsened my humiliation.

Lorraine suggested that we go straight home. I said no. I wanted to continue with our plans to go to Home Depot before returning home.

I have learned with ALS that having some control, even if it's simply going to a store, is important. By that afternoon I had already lost so much: my career, my independence, and now the ability to enjoy a simple hamburger.

Once again, I needed to do "normal" and, for a while, postpone dealing with the day's events.

That day I had taken another step along the deadly path of ALS. For my wife, kids, and me, there'd be no more relaxed meals of eating and chatting.

For the rest of my life, there'd always be that question, "Is Dad OK?"

CHAPTER 4

THE MYSTERY OF THE FIRST GRADE

When I was a toddler, my parents became concerned because I was slow in learning how to speak. They were so concerned that they took me to the doctor, thinking I might be tongue-tied, a condition I do not understand to this day.

The doctor told my parents I didn't need to speak because I had two older siblings who were doing it for me.

Little did my parents know, once I would start speaking, I'd never stop.

After my diagnosis, Lorraine and I traveled to the ALS Clinic at MGH, where I met Dr. Lisa Krivickas for a second opinion. She is now my ALS specialist. During that first visit with her, she told me she had to check my facial muscles and requested that I open my mouth so she could try to shut it.

"Doc, many people have tried that, and no one has ever succeeded," I said.

Then there's the mystery of the first grade. I stayed back.

My mother always maintained that I repeated the first grade because I was ill, but she never told me what I had, giving credence to my siblings' claim that I was "dumb."

In the second grade, I attended Notre Dame School in Springvale. The nuns told me that I had to leave because I spoke English at recess. At this Franco-American school, French was the required language in the playground. I had to transfer to the public school across town, where they spoke English. *C'est la vie!*

Years later, as a freshman at Saint Ignatius High School, I had the honor of taking speech class. Well, I *thought* it was an honor to be selected as a potential speaker, but not so fast. As I realized years later, it was a class for students with speech difficulties.

During my freshman year at the University of Maine, I was in an English class that met four times a week versus the usual three. I figured it was because I came from a small parochial high school and wasn't up to speed.

Decades later, when I was the director of the University College, I kept running into this woman who claimed to have taught me in the third grade at Lincoln School. I don't remember having her as a teacher, but I don't recall whom I did have, so I took her at her word.

One day, we were both in line waiting to order a sandwich at Subway, and she turned to me and mentioned that she "got into a lot of trouble" because of me. She went on to say that she had given me an "A" and apparently you are not supposed to do that in a "remedial class."

Remedial class?

I had gone 50 years not knowing that I had been in a remedial reading class.

Throughout it all, I never figured out that my siblings were probably right.

My denial continued until August 1971. I was taking a course on learning disabilities at the University of Southern Maine. The professor had been going over a variety of disabilities, and on this particular day, he began writing a list of symptoms on the board that had to do with things in series.

He first wrote "difficulty spelling," letters in a series.

I leaned over to the older woman who was sitting next to me and whispered, "If it wasn't for my wife, I couldn't write my lectures for class." I was a history teacher at Kennebunk High School at the time. My classmate smiled.

The professor wrote "difficulty remembering telephone numbers" on the board.

Again, I leaned to my classmate and told her, "Whenever I change my phone number, I can't remember it for months."

Again, she smiled.

My professor added a few more symptoms on the board, and with each challenge I had a related deficiency, each of which I relayed to my classmate next to me. Now others were listening in, and the smiles were spreading across the classroom.

I had to get some answers of my own.

"What about music?" I asked my professor.

He replied, "Music is beats in series," and that someone with this disability would have challenges with it.

At this point, many of my classmates turned to me, having heard my earlier admissions, and waited. I obliged.

"My whole family thinks I'm tone-deaf," I said.

Trying to save face, I asked my professor about languages.

The professor replied, "Ah, words in series."

"I have taken seven years of French and four of Latin," I told him. You could hear the relief from my fellow classmates. But I had to add, "I can't read, write, or translate either one of them today."

At that point, the woman next to me leaned over and asked, "My God, how does it feel at this stage of your life to find out you are learning disabled?"

"Well," I said, "since I'm only two weeks away from my Master's degree, I'm not going to let it bother me."

* * *

Someone once asked me how, given my personal and academic background, I had become the director of not one, but two, college centers within the University of Maine System.

My answer was quick and to the point: "No one ever told me I couldn't."

The naiveté of my youth protected me from having a reason to give up. I had to learn to compensate for my weaknesses and to develop my strengths.

To counter my disability, I had to be inventive and create ways to cope. I had to learn by doing rather than reading. I became involved in everything I could as an adult — from serving on the board of a credit union to better understand finances to being a hospital trustee to garner management experience.

I have served on numerous boards and committees in my 40 years of public and professional life. With each one of them, I have taken away more than I've given.

I have thrived on these experiences and, as a result, my mind is seldom at rest. If I am involved in a meaningless task, my mind will drift over to my creative side in search of answers to just about every question that I can imagine.

I know ALS will take my muscles, but Lou Gehrig's disease generally doesn't affect one's mind — at least not physically. The curse of this dreaded disease is that you are left with your brain intact. Therein lays the challenge: How does someone whose mind is in overdrive survive in a body that has already died?

I Prefer to Laugh

CHAPTER 5

HEAVEN & HELL:
BEEN THERE, DONE THAT

As I adjusted to using a cane, I realized I had lost the spiritual crutch that has sustained me throughout my life.

Since my forehead was anointed with the oils of baptism, I have been a Roman Catholic.

Since my First Communion at age seven, I have been a practicing Catholic, participating in weekly Mass, reciting prayers, and living my life according to the tenets of the Church.

I was so ingrained with Catholicism that I crossed into religious fanaticism at an early age. I was so good at concealing my extremism that few people noticed — until a nun in the fourth grade at Holy Family School told my parents that I needed to see a psychiatrist to address the issue. My folks were financially strapped, but they thought the issue serious enough that they brought me to see a doctor in Portland.

The psychiatrist first spoke separately with my parents. Then, he said to me, "According to your teacher, you always make the Sign of the Cross when you enter or exit the classroom. Why is that?"

"Near each door there's a small container of holy water, and we were told when we pass holy water we should dip our fingers into it and make the Sign of the Cross. I do what I am told," I replied.

He then asked a question I thought was strange.

"How much is a half of a half?"

"A fourth."

After a few other questions, he asked my parents to join us.

The doctor informed my folks that I was fine, and that they should send him my teacher instead. He should have realized that when a nun believes someone is a religious fanatic, there just might be something to it.

He was wrong. I was not fine. I was just good at appearing that way. I was, after all, the son of an alcoholic, the third child, and the youngest. My role was to make people happy.

Adding to the burdens of the family was not in my job description. My struggle with religion would remain private. I was viewed by those who knew me as being a "nice kid," a "do-gooder."

I have always hated mornings and looked forward to sleeping in on the weekends. When I was young, I would force myself to get out of bed to attend the 6:30 a.m. Mass with my mother. On the surface, this appeared to be the deed of a good son, but it was driven by the fear that if I did not get up, my mother would miss Mass and I would be responsible for her sin.

I went beyond the normal round of morning and evening prayers to praying randomly throughout the day for no apparent reason.

I was a child who did not question what I was told but rather accepted things as they were stated.

I believed that I should do no wrong because the consequences would be so dire.

I have come to realize that it was not the fault of my religion but rather the consequence of being raised in a dysfunctional family that led to my extremism.

I needed to believe in something that was definitive, unquestionable.

Catholicism offered that. There was right or wrong — no in between.

In high school, I had some teachers who were secular priests, and I began to view my religion differently. Priests, at least most of the ones I've encountered in high school and beyond, are more open and view life differently than did the sequestered nuns.

I learned that the concept of questioning one's religion is not heresy.

49

With Vatican II, I realized how open my faith could be. The change ushered in by Pope John XXIII allowed me to question my religion as I do everything in my life.

I now believe I am a better Catholic for this.

Over the years, especially as I raised my family, I have succeeded in establishing a healthier balance between religion and life.

I don't regret the kind of person I've become because of my religion, but I do regret the worrying, the guilt, and the struggle that being overly religious brought with it.

As an adult, I have never prayed for monetary rewards, worldly goods, or victorious events. With each morning and evening prayer, with each weekly Mass, I've made one request, for the "health, safety, protection, and happiness of my family."

I realized that there would be illnesses. I was aware of my own mortality; however, I never once imagined that the response to six decades of prayer would be the devastating statement, "You have Lou Gehrig's disease."

ALS is the one disease that will strip me of everything I hold dear. If I had never uttered a word of prayer, never spent a moment in a church, would the outcome had been the same?

The answer is simple. Yes.

I've often heard people say, "God never gives us more than we can handle."

In order to prove the above statement, you must first define "more than." Is it when one collapses mentally and enters an irreversible state, or is death itself the outer limit?

Maybe the statement exists solely as a means of consolation and hope.

* * *

In the spring of 2008, I worked with my personal physician and my ALS specialist to participate in a clinical trial. It was necessary for me to have blood work done to establish a baseline for the study.

My test results indicated an above-normal white-cell count. My doctor felt he needed to run additional tests, the results of which would take a week.

After the tests, Lorraine and I left for a vacation to Atlantic City. On the way home, we stopped in Massachusetts for the night. I decided to call my doctor to see if he had received the results. He had. They were positive for Chronic Lymphocytic Leukemia (CLL).

Days later, I visited my doctor. He asked me if I recalled what I said on the phone when he informed me that I had CLL. I told him I did not.

"You told me you could only die once," he said.

I followed up with an oncologist. Given my CLL's slow progression, we decided that my primary focus should remain with ALS.

As my wife stated, "We have been there, and we are *not* going back." We had dealt with a diagnosis of a terminal illness with ALS, and we had passed through the associated stages of grieving; we were not about to go through it again with CLL.

Once again, I contemplated the belief as to what one can handle as I confronted a second incurable illness.

If one is to assume that God has not given me more than I can handle, then I would also have to believe that God has given me ALS and then piled on by giving me cancer. One cannot believe the former while denying the latter.

I do not believe God gave me ALS or cancer. I believe that life happens without His intervention.

However, I do understand the benefits of the psychology of believing that God answers our prayers.

ALS has taken away my career, my zest for life, and my ability to carry my grandson or kick a soccer ball with my granddaughter.

It has diminished my self-esteem, destroyed my muscles, and taken away my freedom.

I face the future of a drawn-out death by paralysis.

Cancer is not more than I can handle. That milestone was passed with the words, "You have Lou Gehrig's disease."

For most of my adult life, long before the onset of my ALS, I have questioned and eventually rejected the concept of heaven and hell, at least in the traditional sense of their meanings.

My thinking tends to be analytical and dependent on tangible facts. To me, the existence of heaven and hell defies logic. I believe it is human nature to protect oneself by believing the spirit continues even after the body has died. Individuals have difficulty accepting their mortality, so the concept of an afterlife is comforting to them.

As a believer in evolution, I hold the view that we are living creatures with advanced intellects who have developed into the human species we are today.

I *do* believe our spirits live on, but not in the generally accepted definition of where we go once we die.

When I die, I will not visit the Pearly Gates, nor, thank God, the fires of damnation. Rather, my spirit will live through my family; it will be present in what I have done throughout my life.

My spirit will live on in my beloved wife, as she copes with her loss and holds dear the memories we built together as we shaped one another's lives.

My afterlife will not be in a place called heaven or hell. It will exist in my children. Throughout their lives, they have been infused with my influence, positive and not so positive. Their personalities are the results of the tremendous love that we have for each other. Their character reflects those of their parents. Their morals and beliefs have been influenced by their upbringing under my wife's and my guidance.

We are reflections of our parents, of people with whom we come into contact, of the environment in which we have developed, and of the circumstances we have confronted.

I am the result of the love of both of my parents, of the strength of my mother as well as the sins of my father.

I was raised with an alcoholic father whose own self-abuse led to his destruction. I never questioned his love, and I understood his death.

I am very much my father's son. I have the Irish wit, the love of people, and the drive to lead rather than follow. His spirit continues to live on in me and through me in my children and my grandchildren.

I began to break the cycle of my father's alcoholism, and my children have completed that effort, for it is reported that it takes two generations to put an end to that tragic illness.

My challenge in life has been to filter that spirit and carry on the good (heaven) while attempting to negate the bad (hell).

My mother's spirit is likewise present in me. Her spirit is one of heaven: strength, morality, faith, and a positive attitude.

During three years of tragic losses of family and friends, I've often heard the words "we will meet again in heaven" and "our loved ones are watching over us." One might think that these words run counter to my views, but I see them as consistent.

You "meet your loved ones" every time you think of them, for their spirit is truly present in you. They are watching over you, not from above but from within.

I will remain with my family after ALS takes my final breath, for I will live within them through the influences that I have had during my time on earth.

I will look over them by being present in their minds. The way I have lived my life will give them models of what I did right as well as what I did wrong. From those impressions, I will indeed be there in spirit to help them through the challenges of their lives.

As for me, ALS has been my hell; the peace of my passing will be my heaven; and my spirit will live on in the generations to come.

I Prefer to Laugh

CHAPTER 6

THE IRONY OF IT ALL

No one has ever called me athletic, so it did not come as a surprise when, upon hearing about my Lou Gehrig's disease, my brother asked if he was the only one who saw the irony. It was, after all, my brother who was the three-sport athlete with an array of athletic honors and trophies. I was at most a team manager.

More than half a century before I was diagnosed with a disease named after a baseball great, my athletic future, or lack of one, was sealed by none other than my father.

Reluctantly, I tried out for Little League when I was seven years old, even though I was afraid of hard objects speeding directly at me. I had decided to try out because I thought every seven-year-old boy was expected to play ball.

I also lacked the coordination needed to "slide into second." The concept of running at full speed while hurling oneself onto the ground toward a base still eludes me today.

I was relieved when I was cut from the team. Now, more than five decades later, I look back and I am left wondering about the way it happened.

My Dad had driven me to the tryouts, only to cut me from the team. He was the coach. I had to walk home, while he stayed and coached his players. Most fathers coach to be with their children, to nurture them, but not mine.

I have rationalized over the years that Dad knew I didn't want to play and did me a favor.

But reality hit home during the summer of 2007, when Roger Laprise, a dear friend and classmate, dropped by the house to give me an old newspaper clipping he had discovered in his archives. It was a photo of his first day of organized baseball. The picture showed Roger and his coach — a man I immediately recognized as my father.

A few days later, I retold my story about being cut from the team at a barbecue that Roger and I attended. Danny Duchette, another classmate and friend, blurted out that my Dad was also *his* coach.

A month later, Roger was inducted into the Maine Baseball Hall of Fame, and I had the honor of attending the ceremony.

I joked with Roger that there's a strong likelihood that some 50 years later *I* would have been the one being inducted into that prestigious hall of fame. That is, if it were not for my coach.

***

Then there was that old football injury. In the late 1980s, I had to have a knee operation, so I visited a sports medicine physician. After the operation, folks would ask what happened.

I would answer, "It's an old football injury."

To which everyone would respond, "I thought that you were just a manager."

I would simply reply, "Some neighborhood kids were playing with an old football and it hit me in the knee."

***

Despite my inability to participate in anything that involved coordination, it never stopped me from becoming a coach.

In 1968, when I was 23, I received a call while I was home from college on spring break. It was the superintendent of schools in Stonington, which is located off the coast of Maine. He was calling to offer me a teaching position, which I thought strange, since I had not applied there.

He had gotten my name through the University of Maine's education department.

I had not received any other job offers, so I accepted the position of social studies teacher for a starting salary of $5,000.

Just as our conversation drew to a close, he asked, "Can you coach basketball?"

Without hesitating, I said "yes," which was strange, given I have no basketball ability. I could never get the concept of dribbling and running at the same time. However, I was not completely without experience. As I had done with football, I had been the manager of my high school's basketball team.

The superintendent never asked for qualifications, and I never offered any.

How tough could it be? Besides, it was only the jayvee team, and it paid an extra $250.

When I returned to the University, I dropped by the bookstore and in the physical education section I found a book on how to coach basketball.

One game, against Vinalhaven High School, exemplifies my basketball coaching career.

On a cold Saturday morning during the winter of 1970, I reported to the Stonington High School Gym. Stonington is best known for its artists, for being the home of the granite that graces President Kennedy's grave, and for the Stonington High School Mariners basketball team.

On that Saturday, my jayvee basketball team was not scheduled to make the two-and-a-half-hour trip to the island of Vinalhaven for that night's varsity match-up. At the last minute, the home team called and said they would like the jayvees to play before the varsity game. An earlier match-up had been canceled due to high seas.

Our caravan of cars was scheduled to leave within the hour, so time was running out. Our varsity coach decided to play the jayvee game but with the players he had assembled. Since four of my players also played for the varsity, I already had four-fifths of a team. The varsity coach threw in his manager and a player to be named later.

The hour ride to Rockland was uneventful, but I was unprepared for the 90 minutes on the ferry. I had never been out of sight of land before, and my stomach was rolling with the waves.

We arrived at the Vinalhaven wharf and our players disbursed throughout the island to the homes of host families. The varsity coach and I were escorted to a boarding house.

There was no way off the island until morning.

All the coaches and officials dined on beans and franks at the home of Vinalhaven's head coach. The menu was a precursor to what was to come.

In hindsight, I should have taken closer notice that the officials got to spend the night at that same coach's home.

Tip-off time arrived and with it commenced the most unusual basketball game I have ever experienced. I warned my small band of six players to be careful about fouls because our bench of one gave us very little depth. Unfortunately, the two officials, fueled by their earlier dinner, proved to be full of hot air.

By halftime, my five starters had amassed a large number of fouls. Halfway through the third period, my first player fouled out. I looked at my bench and the decision was easy. It was time to send in the only one sitting there – the varsity player on loan from the head coach.

He immediately made an impression on the fans, all of whom were from Vinalhaven, by outplaying the less experienced jayvee players. This raised the question in many minds as to why a coach would not put in his best player until the second half. Nobody from Vinalhaven knew he was a "ringer" whom I was trying to save for the varsity game.

I pleaded with my team not to foul out, but the officials, hoping for a good night's sleep, would have none of it. Five minutes into the final period, the whistle blew again and another of my players bit the dust. I looked at my bench, and then I looked at the refs and I shrugged. Since we were ahead, they allowed the game to continue — Vinalhaven's five against my four.

Seconds later, another whistle, and it was three against five.

By now the Vinalhaven fans had switched sides, cheering wildly for their opposition, much to the dismay of their coach, who saw little humor in the situation, especially since his team was still behind.

You can imagine how the gymnasium erupted when yet another whistle was blown, and I was down to my final two — the manager and the varsity loaner. I called a time-out and switched to a new strategy: a two-on-five defense, our man-to-man had died several questionable calls earlier. I again pleaded with my remaining players not to foul because we were remarkably still in the game, and we now had a gymnasium full of supporters, none of whom we knew.

Then came one final blast of hot air passing through the referee's lips and into his whistle — our manager had fouled out.

The officials, with their first logical call of the evening, declared the game over because my "loan" player had no one to whom he could pass the ball. We lost the game by a score of 65 to 62, with 33 seconds left on the board.

My career as a high school coach ended when I accepted a teaching position in Kennebunk in 1970.

* * *

I have never let my lack of athletic ability interfere with my coaching.

In 1980, I asked my son, Shawn, who was eight at the time, what sport he would like to play. He replied "soccer," which proved to be a challenge, since there was no youth soccer program in our community.

Undeterred, I called the coach of the high school soccer team, Peter Levasseur, whom I did not know, and asked if he would be interested in starting a soccer association in town.

In less than six weeks, we had 120 boys and 12 teams, uniforms and all. The next year, we expanded the soccer association to include girls. Eventually, my daughter, Kelly, would play in that same program, and Lorraine would coach her.

Today, more than 25 years later, the Sanford-Springvale Soccer Association has close to 700 players, making it the largest in Maine.

In 2007, I felt great pride when I watched my granddaughter, Madeline, play in her first team sport. She joined the association's "Little Kickers," a program for four-years-olds that introduces them to soccer. The next year, she was on the Sleeper's Market team, which was coached by her dad, the boy for whom the program was created.

* * *

Before anyone thinks my life has been completely devoid of any physical activity, I should point out that I was in shape once. In 1965, at the end of my freshman year at college, I needed to test out of physical education or repeat it during my sophomore year.

In high school, I was fortunate because college-prep students didn't have time in their schedules and were, therefore, exempt from taking P.E.

So I decided to cram for the test. For two weeks, I went to the gym and practiced chin-ups; I ran on the track to improve my speed; and, in my dorm room, I performed sit-ups until I could meet the minimum standard for passing out of physical education.

The big day came, and I barely passed the required exercises. It was the only day in my 64 years that I can say I was in good physical shape. The way I view it: *Accomplished it, moved on!*

As my non-athletic career comes to an end, I am faced with yet another sports irony.

On August 4, 2008, the first annual Gary Sullivan ALS Golf Tournament was held at the Old Marsh Golf Course in Wells, Maine. The course is new, and the event was the first public function to be held there. A dear friend, Ted Hissong, and his corporation, The Hissong Group, sponsored the tournament. The event raised $25,000 for the fight to strike out ALS.

And yes, I do not play golf.

At this point, my brother — the athlete and avid golfer, but, I might add, not a soccer player — rants at every new development in my athletic career.

The real irony is that while ALS ended Lou Gehrig's sports career, it launched mine. I have finally become associated with one of baseball's greats. He and I share a league of our own — we're pALS.

Oh, the irony of it all!

I Prefer to Laugh

CHAPTER 7

THAT PREGNANT GUY

One night, during a thunderstorm, I watched an episode of "Grey's Anatomy." It was the one about the husband who was pregnant.

Halfway through the show, tears started rolling down my cheeks.

I'm pretty sure it wasn't the pregnant guy's fault.

Maybe it was exhaustion. During the previous two weeks, I had been to Massachusetts General Hospital in Boston three times and had spent three days helping my daughter and her husband move into their new home. I was at the end of a weekend during which my family and friends built a new, handicapped accessible bathroom on the first floor of my home.

Maybe I was overwhelmed with gratitude towards my friends and family, for whom the project to build the bathroom

67

was truly a labor of love to which they gave their time, energy, and support.

Or maybe it was seeing my home altered forever to accommodate what was to come.

Or, just maybe, it was all of the above, minus the pregnant father, that brought tears to my eyes on that rainy Sunday night.

Forty-one years had passed since my classmates and I graduated from high school. Over the years our class has remained close, because my first prom date and good friend, Anne Marie Mosher, has taken the lead in coordinating social events for all of us to attend.

As a result of this closeness, my fellow classmates once again surrounded me on that November weekend nearly one year after my diagnosis.

Upon hearing about my condition, Roger Laprise came to my home and offered his help.

Camille Walsh offered her husband, Dave, and he graciously agreed and even got their son, James, into the act.

Bob LaFrance, my close friend of more than 50 years, came up from Newburyport, Massachusetts, to help with the work. Our home of 34 years, after all, was where Dottie, Bob's wife, was raised. She was also a classmate. It was her homestead we were altering.

Danny Duchette heard about it and showed up, ready to work.

It was a solemn occasion for me. I have lived in the same house since 1971. Lorraine and I moved there six months after we got married. I had always been the one to renovate our house; however, on that weekend in November 2005, I was an observer to the most radical changes in my home since the outhouse was moved from the back yard to the second floor, well before my time.

My lack of strength prevented me from doing any physical labor. That, and several tall guys with hammers, made it clear I would not be lifting a finger that day. They were there to help their friend and classmate.

My son, Shawn, and son-in-law, Jay, also joined the construction crew.

Our good friends, Perry and Louise Wood, neither of whom have ever claimed to be handy with a hammer, arrived at noon with a large batch of spaghetti and homemade meatballs with all the fixings to feed our small army of volunteers.

But it was the dessert that proved to be special. It was chocolate chip cookies. Not just any chocolate chip cookies; these came from Goodall Hospital's cafeteria.

When I was a trustee at the hospital, I would look forward to board meetings because there was always a batch of those special cookies waiting for us.

It was not the chocolate chips that made those cookies special that day; it was that Perry and Louise purposely went out of their way to get them.

69

I think it was a combination of factors that brought me to tears that night: the close support and loving relationships and the realization that the house, my home, was being altered to accommodate the anticipated arrival of the paralysis that is ALS.

OK, maybe just one of the tears was for that pregnant guy on "Grey's Anatomy."

* * *

Several months later, after we completed the bathroom and built an addition onto my study, which was to become our bedroom, I was once again brought to tears.

Shawn, Kelly, and Jay had moved our furniture from our upstairs bedroom of 35 years to the first floor next to our new handicap-accessible bathroom.

After Lorraine went to bed that evening, I climbed the stairs to our former bedroom. The room was bare.

I slowly walked to where our bed had been, laid on the floor and wept.

We had moved our bedroom not because we wanted to renovate but because we were forced to — our circumstances required it.

The view from our bed overlooking our street would never be the same. The sounds of traffic in that front room had been replaced by quieter ones at the back of the house.

I found myself mourning yet another loss of "normalcy."

* * *

Ever since the kids left for college, I have not been able to eat at the dining room table, except when they come home to visit or we have company. Many wonderful moments took place around that table as the four of us would dine and talk about the day's events.

Now Lorraine and I have dinner while watching television in our living room, and I eat with my plate on my lap. On one occasion, my plate jumped and I looked at my leg and thought, "Don't you dare."

My muscles were twitching as if they were dancing to a symphony.

It was the night before Valentine's Day, and my legs were under attack. There were twitches from my thighs to my feet.

The twitches are called fasciculations. With my learning disability, I can never remember that word and, of course, I can never spell it. So when I told my ALS specialist I was having "flatulations," she knew what I meant, and it provided some much-needed comic relief.

That February night, the fasciculations had returned with a vengeance. Each twitch made me realize that the rest of my legs were fighting a losing battle.

I had been fasciculation-free for some time. Oh, there had been the occasional twitch, but my limbs had been relatively quiet for several months.

A few days later, as I went to get out of bed, I paused, and sat on the edge with my feet dangling, not quite reaching the floor. I had noticed over the past 26 months the slow erosion of my muscle mass, especially in my legs.

But that day my feet looked different. They just hung there, with no muscles to hold them up. I was surprised because my right foot had been the only part of my body to offer no resistance during a recent exam at my specialist's office.

Everything had happened so gradually I had not noticed how bad my right foot had gotten. My big toe had dropped, and I had very little control over the movement in my right foot. It had, for all practical purposes, died.

* * *

Through the use of leg braces, I am still able to walk. They serve as artificial muscles that hold my feet in place.

I do notice that my balance is worse when I do not wear my braces. I do well, mind you, but I have fallen a few times and bumped my head on the floor. My balance gets better as mornings progress, but my difficulties return during the evenings, as my muscles grow tired from the day's activities.

I know I will lose my ability to walk, to stand, and to drive when my legs permanently weaken.

These days, my reality is that I'm not as healthy as I look at this stage of my illness.

I intentionally try to hide the signs of my disease. It is the Irish in me. I am stubborn and proud, and I use humor to face the challenges of life.

My pants hide the braces that wrap around my calves and run down into my shoes, extending at right angles to the tips of my toes.

These braces allow me to walk. At home, when I take them off, I slowly walk around from room to room, bouncing from one piece of furniture to another, occasionally touching a wall with my shoulder to maintain my balance.

The human body is amazing. We seldom stop to think how well proportioned it is until it begins to change. I never would have expected that a dropped foot could put my toes out of the reach of my arms. As I struggle to put on my stockings, the reality of that proportion hits home.

While my loss of weight is noticeable, down to 157 pounds from a high of 184, the loss of muscle mass is hidden.

Jerseys cover my shoulders, which have lost all human padding. When I touch them, I feel the distinct angles of my bones.

There are times when my right hand, especially the thumb and the finger next to it, lock into a position over which I have no control. I quickly massage my arm with my left hand, alleviating the limited paralysis, and the sharp pain that accompanies it.

When I shave I see my eyes in the mirror and the quivering muscles just below them.

Taking a shower is a cruel reminder of the ravages of ALS. Increasingly, my body is becoming a skeleton with a layer of skin.

The disease has progressed, and I am sicker than I will allow myself to show.

I used to look forward to meals. I love food, and I enjoyed socializing with family and friends while I ate, either at home or at a restaurant. Now eating is a task — small bites, endless chewing and then a hopeful swallow, capped with a swig of water to wash it down. The pleasures of a simple meal are gone.

A meal that once took me 20 minutes to enjoy now takes 45 to get through. At restaurants, wait staff always clear off everyone else's plates when they finish, leaving me as the sole person at the table who still has an unfinished meal in front of him. It's embarrassing and, as a result, I simply stop eating and push my plate away.

I do go out to pubs with three of my classmates, Roger, Danny, and Ray Beaudoin. We call ourselves the ROMEOs — Retired Old Men Eating Out. I enjoy these meals because they last three hours and the guys watch out for me without making it seem or feel like they are.

Many friends have asked me how I deal with my ALS and the future that awaits me.

I reply that I only have two choices, to laugh or to cry. I prefer to laugh. Without laughter, I could not endure life, for under the disguise of my clothes, there is a body and a mind struggling to survive.

CHAPTER 8

THE "TALK"

During the summer of 2006, Lorraine saw my foot and made a comment as I sat on the edge of our bed. She noticed that the little toe and the one next to it had started to drop on my left foot — a new development and an unwelcome one.

There was no more denying the inevitable. The process of my paralysis was under way, one digit at a time.

A few days later, I went to the hospital to visit a friend and fellow hospital trustee who was gravely ill.

Upon entering his room, I said, "Hi Scottie, it's Gary."

My friend's eyes opened wide, and he replied in a strong voice, "Hi," but I could tell it was more of a reaction than an acknowledgement.

The next morning, he died of pancreatic cancer.

The same day that Scottie Hoar passed away, my daughter and son-in-law had come to town to help me with some yard work. Crab grass had taken over our walkway, our shrubs were sprouting out in all directions, and our lawn had become a hayfield. Things had come to that because I had refused to accept my loss of energy; as a result, I had not asked anyone for help with our yard.

In the afternoon, I heard a noise coming from inside the house. Jay told me that he thought that my wife was crying. I walked as quickly as my tired limbs would permit me. My wife was standing by the phone in tears. Her sister's husband, our brother-in-law, had been diagnosed with cancer — pancreatic cancer.

Once again, we were pushed to the brink.

Once again, we struggled to comprehend the unthinkable.

Once again, we caught our breath.

The next day, we received an e-mail from my son's dear friend, a mother of triplets, whose family is considered part of our extended family. The e-mail stated, "I am just writing to let you know that Dad passed away this morning. He is now at peace and no longer suffering."

The e-mail continued with the details of the wake, the funeral Mass, and the gathering afterwards. It concluded, "Please continue to keep us in your prayers during this difficult time."

Cause of death: pancreatic cancer.

Three days, two deaths, one new diagnosis, and three grieving families.

Somehow, my "little toes that couldn't" didn't seem as important in the realm of things. Somehow, the paralysis at that point was tolerable, especially when compared to the horrible grief of those three families.

* * *

Nearly four years after the onset of my disease, these three developments regarding pancreatic cancer made me realize that it was time to have "the talk" with my personal physician, a friend who had difficulty accepting the diagnosis of ALS.

My doctor of 23 years had retired, and I was searching for a new one when people I respect suggested I wait. They told me the person chosen to fill my doctor's vacancy came highly recommended. I'm glad I waited; years later, Dr. Bhargava proved to be the right physician for me as I faced the greatest health crisis of my life.

Dr. Mukesh Bhargava and I became friends while working on improving medical services in our community. I was a hospital trustee at the time, and he was a new physician who was putting down roots in the community

One afternoon, as Mukesh and I left a meeting, he took me aside and said he wanted me to see a different doctor for my cholesterol. I asked why. He told me he disagreed with my decision not to care about it.

I replied, "I don't want another doctor, and I *don't* care about my cholesterol."

"But I do, and I'm concerned that you could have a heart attack."

"But I *want* a heart attack."

"I don't lose many folks to heart attacks with all the new treatments," he said.

With my Irish humor, I said, "What good are you!"

Months later, I told Dr. Bhargava about the tightness of the muscles in my jaw, which caused difficulty chewing and strain after long periods of speaking. I asked him if the tightness was the result of my stress from dealing with ALS.

He asked to see my tongue. After a good look, he told me that the tightness was not stress-related. My tongue was now showing signs of atrophy and fasciculation.

In other words, it was ALS, not stress.

Mukesh had been the one who kept open the possibility that my ALS diagnosis could have been wrong. He would admit to me later that it was not the physician who could not accept the diagnosis, but the friend who did not want to.

But on that summer day any last ray of hope disappeared. I returned home and went to my bedroom. My son stopped by the house and came into the room. For the first time since the early days of my disease, I fell apart. I collapsed crying in his arms.

That was my last good cry. For some reason, unknown to me, I have not been able to cry like that since. There are times when I want to, but it is like all the tears are gone.

* * *

On my next visit, I decided to have "the talk" with my physician and friend, Dr. Bhargava.

I began by telling him that I understand that I will most likely die from choking or respiratory failure. I asked if I would need an oxygen tube to help me breathe.

He said no. He explained that the muscles necessary to inhale the oxygen also will die.

I had told Dr. Bhargava, early on, that I *would not* have a tracheotomy. *That* is emphatically spelled out in my Advanced Medical Directive.

After I left Dr. Bhargava's office, I reflected on our conversation and realized I had not asked him if I would be left gasping for air without a tracheotomy.

At my next appointment, three months later, I asked him about it.

His reply was comforting.

"No," he said. "I would not let that happen. You would go under palliative care."

Palliative care is designed to improve the quality of life for patients and families who need end-of-life care.

I have had a great life. I am not interested in extending it beyond the point when its quality has been taken away.

My step-dad lost his battle against Alzheimer's. When I think of him, his final days, not the quality of his earlier years, come to mind.

CHAPTER 9

LEGACY

As I begin my seventh year since the onset of my ALS, I am brought back to the night of my diagnosis. Our family gathered in the same home where both kids were raised and where they had spent their childhoods in a safe and warm environment. We sat around the living room, as we had done so many times before. It was in this room where Christmas gifts were opened, Easter Eggs were searched for, and endless hours of family memories were shared.

However, on this day, the mood was different. We were talking about the unknown.

Kelly, whose wedding was ten months away, asked, "Will you be able to walk me down the aisle?"

Shawn stated that he wanted his 20-month-old daughter, Madeline, to know her "Grampy."

* * *

81

June 9, 1975.

The time, 1:50 p.m.

My daughter had entered the world. A bouquet of flowers displayed in her room read, "Thanks to a wonderful wife and welcome to Daddy's Little Girl."

Thirty years later, on my sixtieth birthday, I would see that card again, below a picture of my daughter as an infant. This time, the card was an image that was part of a "memory quilt" that my daughter had made.

Twenty-five days later, my daughter would be married. Right after my diagnosis, she had moved up her wedding date in the hopes I could be there.

Since the day Kelly Elizabeth Sullivan was born, I had looked forward to walking my daughter down the aisle and to dancing with her to the music of "Daddy's Little Girl" by Bobby Burke & Horace Gerlach.

On July 9, 2005, I walked my little girl down the aisle and later danced with her to that very song.

As fate would have it, during her wedding reception, guests came in from the deck of the hall and asked us to join them. There, over the treetops, was a rainbow, and my daughter was its pot of gold.

Not only did I live to see Kelly's wedding, I was there a year and a half later for the birth of her son, my grandson, Rowen Sullivan Shafer. He has helped to make my life complete, as he brings joy into his Mem and Grampy's lives.

* * *

During the spring of 2005, I sat down to write my thoughts regarding my son's concern that his daughter would not grow up knowing her "Grampy."

When I began writing, I had no idea where my thoughts would take me. When I finished, I knew everything was going to be OK.

> *According to my neurologist, two years ago was the time of the onset of my disease.*
>
> *Two years ago, that was the time of one of the happiest moments of my life: the birth of my granddaughter.*
>
> *Two years ago, one life began, another began to decline.*
>
> *Two years ago, my granddaughter entered this world as her grandfather, unknowingly, began to leave it.*
>
> *For two years, a child has learned to walk, to hold, to speak.*
>
> *For two years, a man has begun to stumble, to lose his grip, to monitor his speech.*
>
> *As one develops her personality, the other struggles to maintain his.*

As the child moves toward the start of her education, the man leaves behind a life dedicated to education.

The grandfather hopes to see his granddaughter play soccer in the very program he started, 25 years earlier, for her dad.

The grandfather hopes that the changes in the medical environment of his community, as his nine years as a hospital trustee comes to an end, will provide his granddaughter with state-of-the-art medical care.

Grampy, a director of the town's community center and chair of its theatre renovations, hopes that time is on his side to complete the project so that his granddaughter may participate in artistic and cultural endeavors.

Two years after her birth, two years after the onset of his disease, the grandfather is not saddened by the confluence of events but gratified by them. The passing of one generation to another is natural. For a grandfather to have been able to help shape the community in which his dear Maddie will live can only be really appreciated by the "Grampy" who will eventually move on . . .

***

While serving on boards, committees, and commissions has been an important part of my life, it has never been my primary focus. That has always been reserved for my family.

It is through my family that my true legacy will live on.

The legacy of my professional life will be carried forward by my daughter, who is a better teacher than I ever dreamt of being.

The legacy of my public life will continue through my son, an award-winning editor and a volunteer with local committees and organizations.

The legacy of my private life will remain in the heart of my best friend and wife.

The legacy of my very being will be carried on for generations by two special people: Madeline Avonlea Sullivan and Rowen Sullivan Shafer.

Knowing all of this gives me great comfort and peace and the ability to accept my fate.

I have a new philosophy: "It is important in life to take the time to stop and smell the grandchildren. It is not always pleasant, but it is always a great joy!"

* * *

I have come to realize what ALS is. It is a journey back in life — a return to infancy.

As nights deepen, I walk around my home realizing my steps are numbered. I get a sense of a clicker counting down my final movements, ultimately replacing my legs with wheels. Then the counter resets, and the countdown of rotations begins until all motion ceases.

These are the thoughts that go through my head as another day ends. I have no sense of how many steps remain in the counter because no one can read the numbers, only the signs: fewer stairs climbed; slower pace of walking; lessened stability. Neurons die while others struggle to pick up the load, leading to increased fatigue and decreased energy.

It is as if a mathematical formula has taken over my life. There is no way to control the formula and the resulting numbers from descending. I work on what I can control: making the most of the number of hours I am awake; enjoying a simple lunch with friends; the company of family; a laugh with my wife. I can enjoy the warmth of the day or the soothing sound of rain. I can revisit the bright memories of my past while lying to rest the discomforting ones.

For as long as my remaining neurons are working overtime, I have some control over the mathematics of my days. While the hours will run out each night, if I, rather than ALS, have controlled the day, then I will have a good start with which to meet the dead of night.

The things I learned in my early childhood, the foundations upon which all things are built, I now have to learn to function without.

My first words, then sentences, and eventually whole conversations were met with excitement and joy. Now I am faced with losing the ability to carry on conversations, then speaking in sentences and, eventually, uttering even simple words. ALS will take it all away, as the muscles that perform those functions whither and die due to a lack of neuron stimulation.

There were my first steps, welcomed by my parents and family with the same joy and excitement.

Eventually, steps turned into walking, and walking into running. That process is likewise being reversed.

It has been years since I could run, months since I could walk without support. I now walk with two braces and a rolling cane. The cane will eventually be replaced with a walker, the walker with a wheelchair, and the wheelchair with a bed, and my journey back to infancy will be complete.

Unlike a child learning new things, I am faced with learning how to live without those basic functions. I once learned as an infant to the joy and delight of others. The journey back is being greeted with sadness and despair.

As I took my first breath on June 14, 1945, so too will I depart on a day when I lose that very first function a child does naturally upon exiting the womb — the ability to breath.

I Prefer to Laugh

SECTION II

ONE FAMILY

I Prefer to Laugh

CHAPTER 10

DADDY'S LITTLE GIRL
A Daughter's Perspective

By Kelly Elizabeth Shafer

It is ironic that Dad asked me to write a chapter for his book, since he knows from experience that writing is not something that I like to do. I have memories of kneeling beside his recliner as he helped me with my homework, red pen in hand, and his face almost matching the color of the ink due to his frustration with my lack of writing skills. His voice rose as time went on and my confusion increased.

I don't enjoy writing. I always say that my brother sucked all the good writing genes from my parents when he was born. I also don't enjoy the thought of taking my thoughts and feelings and putting them on display. I am quite happy keeping them to myself or sharing them only with those close to me. I guess I'm like my mother in that respect. When I do share my feelings, it's usually through humor, which I definitely get from my Dad and my grandmother.

So to write a chapter for my Dad's book is a big favor to ask. But for all that my Dad has done for me in my 34 years of life, I guess it's the least I can do for him.

To be true to myself, however, I'll keep most of my most personal feelings private while sharing some stories about someone very special to me…my father.

My Dad and I were always close. We went to car and flower shows together. He helped me learn how to drive. He helped me with financial questions. He even tried to learn how to play tennis, since this was one of my great interests when I was younger. My Dad, who is almost six feet tall, but mostly leg, was the most ungraceful tennis player. His racquet in hand would go one way, while his leg would go the other. To any high schooler, this might be a bit embarrassing, but it was my Dad, and he was trying to show some interest in my life.

I depend on my Dad for lots of things, like daughters do. I always call him for help or suggestions. Even when he didn't have the answer, he would make something up, and I would generally believe anything that he said. When I was in high school, for example, Dad told me he placed first in the high jump, and I bragged to all my friends. He told me years later that he never did the high jump. He had been pulling my leg.

My parents have always made the most of what they had. They worked hard to take us on vacations every year. They made holidays special with traditions. They helped us financially when they really couldn't. They supported my brother and me when we changed colleges, when I wanted to move across the country, and when we changed jobs.

There was the time that I was left on a bus in Washington, D.C., when I was young. My parents and my brother got off the bus first and then the doors closed with me inside, and the bus drove off with my family in hot pursuit.

Patience is not one of Dad's stronger qualities. There was that time at Mount Vernon, home of George Washington, when Dad threw away my unfinished ice cream cone because he was ready to move on and I was eating too slowly.

Once, he picked up my ball while mini-golfing because it was taking me too long to get it in the hole.

Mom and Dad tried to expose us to all sorts of different things. For example, we would stay at a fancy hotel and sip Shirley Temples during cocktail hour for the experience.

I was not punished much as a child; I didn't really require it like my brother did. So on the rare occasion when I did do something wrong, I was always amazed at the punishment put in place for me.

Once I got grounded from touching my cat for a week – no one knows what I did that required such a harsh punishment. Dad says it must have been something pretty bad because he knew how much I loved Lucky.

Then there was the time he charged me money when I left the oven on after making him bread pudding. I made it for him, and he made me pay for it. His excuse was that it was the second time I had left the oven on, and I needed to pay for the electricity. By the way, my Uncle Butch gave me 35 cents on the day of my wedding, apparently feeling sorry for me after all those years.

Whenever Dad is around, things are always interesting. One of the things my father does best is tell stories. Everyone who knows him knows that he is gifted in that respect. He can make anyone laugh, and most of the time it is at his own expense. That's not easily done, but somehow in his life he has mastered it.

As he got a little older, we weren't sure if it was that his memory was going or if he was running out of material, but he started repeating his stories more and more. It was at the *ALS Walk* when my brother and I decided that if Dad told the Wal-Mart story one more time we would have to stage an intervention. He then went on to tell the crowd about how the doctor asked him what his weight was, and he replied, "I weigh about 170 with no clothes on; that is, if the scale in front of Wal-Mart is correct."

I take pride in knowing that I have inherited many of my dad's qualities, such as his sense of humor (a true Irishman never lets the truth stand in the way of a good story); Type A personality that drives my mother nuts; stubbornness; love of learning; independence; eyes that change color depending on what we're wearing; and love for shopping. If I am to include everything, there is also the Sullivan triple chin and very unattractive legs.

Because of our many similarities, most of the time my Dad and I understand each other. We always give each other a hard time, and on a day when we can't laugh or we take things too seriously, we know that something is wrong. I am also proud when I see that I have passed some of these traits on to my son.

Lately, I do make more decisions on my own without my father's input or advice. It's not that he wouldn't help, but I am older, and, I like to think, wiser now. I remember buying a car the day before my son, Rowen, was born. It felt so strange to make such a big decision without my Dad there. But also, my Dad can no longer bear the weight of his children's world on his shoulders like he used to. His physical activity is so much more limited than it was before.

What we used to consider a pretty happy, normal life has taken a different shape now. Our happiness is centered on the children, Rowen and Maddie. We make more of the time we do have together. The things we do now are different. We all take things slower, give in a little easier, and worry a lot more.

However, not one day goes by that I don't consider us blessed. To have had the time we have been granted makes us so much more fortunate than some others. Upon first learning of my Dad's diagnosis, almost four-and-a-half years ago, we never thought that we would have the opportunities we have had. At the time, I was planning for my wedding, and the thought of children was nowhere in sight. Unsure if my father would be able to walk me down the aisle, Jay and I scrambled to change our wedding date, location, theme, and other things. Fortunately, my Dad did walk me down the aisle with support from just a leg brace.

There was also the concern that my children would never know who their grandfather was. Fortunately, my son, Rowen, was born on January 7, 2007, and his Grampy was there at the hospital to greet him. You should see Rowen's eyes light up when he sees his grandfather. He truly loves his "Bampy," and the feeling is mutual. It is a love that has grown over the time that we have been lucky enough to have together.

Humor is a big part of who my father is — whether he was leaving his school pictures under the toilet lid to surprise us in the morning, sending postcards of himself to us in college, or taking a strength test at the Oklahoma State Fair just to see me crack a smile.

A puppy trainer once told me to keep my father away from my dog, Brogan, because he was teaching him bad behaviors. Within the first few moments of visiting my parents, my father would have two bloody ears from playing a little too rough with the puppy. I always chalked it up to my Dad's big ears.

And there is our annual shopping trip the day after Thanksgiving, when the two of us hit the malls together. It always turns into a competition as to who can outlast whom. One year, when I was eight months pregnant, he bragged about winning the "Limp and Blimp" contest. I told him he cheated by using artificial support. He countered by saying that I had two people on my team.

At the beginning he made light of situations and laughed at himself, even though he was realizing that he was sick, way before any doctor could properly diagnose him. Whether he couldn't get up off the floor after genuflecting at church or tripped and fell into the arms of a complete stranger in the freezer aisle at the grocery store, he managed to laugh.

Some days though, it is harder to find humor in it all for my Dad. He does a good job of bouncing back, but some days are just better than others. Something like dropping his phone into my toilet would have been funny years ago, but now it is just an everyday frustration with his weaker, more fumbled movements, and his forgetfulness with all that is on his mind.

Sometimes it just takes a little while for him to see the humor in things. A vibrating, torn apart toilet helps.

I have tried to pay my parents back for all they've done. My brother and I paid some of a trip to Paris for their 25th wedding anniversary. I made my Dad a quilt that reflected his life for his 60th birthday. The truth is that I will never be able to repay them for all they have done; the best repayment is for them to see that I provide similar encouragement and support for my own son.

I remember being at one of Dad's doctor's appointments and hearing him say, "If I could die tomorrow of a heart attack, I would." That was hard to hear, especially because I was pregnant at the time, but I can't fault him for it.

Despite the sadness, the worries, and the dread for what lies ahead, I do feel blessed. All my life, I have been surrounded by people who love me and whom I love dearly. The love of family and friends is what will help me to get though the days that are yet to come. It is those people who will give me the strength to do my job as a mom, a wife, a daughter, a sister, an aunt, a daughter-in-law, and a sister-in-law.

I don't think of the future often because it does me no good now and, to be honest, it is just more than I can bear. At times, my mind starts to wander, and I have become good at bringing myself back to the moment. I try to enjoy the time that we have with my Dad now, watching the love between a grandfather and a grandson grow more with each day.

For now I use what my father gave me — a sense of humor — to deal with this disease that has changed my father and our lives so much. My husband and I joke that we probably won't read this book. We will just wait for the movie of it to come out on Lifetime or USA, right between "Teen Wolf" and "The Breakfast Club." After all, it is my job to keep my father humble!

CHAPTER 11

RIGHT-HAND MAN
A Son's Perspective

By Shawn Patrick Sullivan

Dr. Bhargava slid his hands up and down my lower right leg and settled on the crook behind my knee.

"Okay," he told me. "Put your hand right here, behind your knee, and feel around."

I cupped my hand behind my knee and kneaded my fingers.

"All right," he said. "Do you feel some pudginess there?"

"Sure," I answered.

"You're not supposed to. You're supposed to feel a solid angle there."

I had made an appointment with Dr. Bhargava because I had been troubled by a sensation in my lower right leg and foot. Both had that persistent tingling you feel when your leg or foot is falling asleep. The sensation had been strong enough in recent days that I had to get up from my desk at work and take a few walks around the block.

Dr. Bhargava continued. He explained that the crook in my right knee, with all of its fleshiness, would press flush against the edge of my swivel chair when I sat there at work. As a result of such pressure, the circulation in my leg would get out of whack, and I'd get that bothersome falling-asleep feeling. If I lost a bit of weight, that pudginess would leave the crook of my knee, the undue pressure on my chair would disappear, and my leg would be just fine, Dr. Bhargava said.

"You don't have ALS," he told me, out of the blue.

There you have it. Dr. Bhargava knew why I was *really* there to see him.

Intellectually, I *knew* I did not have ALS. When you're a child of someone with ALS, though, intellect has nothing to do with anything. Every time your foot catches, your balance falters, or your hands fumble, there's a faint voice taunting you from the back of your mind that makes you wonder: *Do I have it too?*

And if not now, will I ever? For me — and for my sister and, thank God, my daughter and my nephew — the answer is likely "no." My father has the sporadic form of ALS, the kind that seemingly strikes from out of nowhere, with no genetic or ancestral traces. If he had had the familial form of ALS, then perhaps this chapter would have been something altogether different.

I hope here to pay tribute to my father, my hero, but my primary goal in these following pages is to show you what it's like to be the child of a parent with Lou Gehrig's disease. If you're a son or daughter who has a parent who has ALS, or has lost a parent to this dreadful illness, and you nod your head here and think, yes, *that's* what it feels like, then I will have succeeded.

Earlier in this book, my father, an educator, says that ALS is largely academic for him during the day. During the night, the disease becomes personal for him, but when the sun's out ALS is something he can discuss and attack by mobilizing people who can help by raising funds and awareness.

For me, it's personal — of course it is; this disease is *killing* my father. More than anything, though, the situation is an emotional one. There is no academic angle for me.

It has been that way from the start. In the days that followed Dad's diagnosis, my sister surfed the Internet to absorb the science of the disease. I headed to the bookstore in search of a biography about Lou Gehrig. I also bought a copy of Christopher Reeve's memoir, "Still Me." I was grateful when I broke the news about Dad to my childhood friend, and he mailed me a copy of Lance Armstrong's book, in which the cyclist shares his experiences with fighting testicular cancer.

I wanted to absorb inspiring stories about how others dealt with diseases and paralysis.

My sister, Kelly, and I take turns accompanying Mom and Dad to Massachusetts General Hospital in Boston when Dad has an appointment with his ALS specialist. My sister, an educator like my father, would find it fascinating when Dad's doctor would test the strength of his feet, legs, arms, shoulders, and jaw. I found such sights unbearable; while I remained completely composed, it broke my heart and angered me to see my father sitting nervously without a shirt in a doctor's office and being "poked and prodded" to gauge his vanishing strength and abilities.

As a son — as *his* son — I've had a difficult time allowing myself the luxury of standing apart from Dad and regarding him as his own, separate person. I've had difficulty seeing myself as such too. As a child and a teenager, it was never an issue; I was a carefree and confident kid who enjoyed good times. As an adult, however, I have always been acutely aware that I am an extension of my father, somebody tied to him both by genetics and the shared desires to serve, achieve, and help leave our hometown better than we found it.

When I was fresh out of college, without a plan, this connection cast over me a shadow deep and dark enough to make me feel blurred and erased. Such pressures were self-imposed; both my father and mother have always given my sister and me the freedom to be and do what we want, on our own terms and on our own timetables. My father stands tall in my life, but there has always been abundant sunshine all around me. As a younger man, I chose to stand in Dad's shadow, rather than step into the sunlight, because I admired him and aspired to be like him.

Now that I'm older, though, and established and successful on my own professional and personal terms, I no longer feel like I'm in anyone's shadow. I do, however, still manage to let the father-son dynamic trip me up, oftentimes when it comes to ALS.

When I deal with my father as a father, I am often taken aback when he shares or presses his evolving attitudes towards such matters as faith and politics; so much of it seems different or contradictory from the way he expressed himself when he was charged with the responsibility of raising my sister and me. While Dad has always had opinions, ALS has made him more assertive and emphatic.

However, when I see my father as an individual — when I am able to extricate myself from our deep family ties — I appreciate him better as his own person, on his own journey, with his own discoveries and desires to chart his own course and control his own destiny. I am a better son, and easier to get along with, when I'm able to regard Dad this way.

When ALS reared its reprehensible head in 2004, it magnified the issues I needed to resolve so that I could emerge as my own man. I realized that my world, so complete with my wife, Valerie, and our daughter, Madeline, was nonetheless paternal-centric. My mind centered on my father.

Imagine what would happen to all of us if one day the sun disappeared and left nothing but cold and darkness in its wake. Now you know how I felt when I learned ALS would be removing my father from my universe. My accomplishments become real once I share them with Dad, and he beams with pride. Jokes are funnier with him there to tell them or laugh at them. Problems seem smaller and manageable when he applies common sense and wisdom to the advice he offers.

ALS forced me to break down my mind and rebuild it. I have made enormous strides, all for the better, but it is an effort that continues to this day. Like all sons and daughters, especially those with parents with terminal illnesses, I must prepare for the day when my father, one of my best friends, is no longer here.

It's coming. Dad's ALS is progressing slowly, but the accumulation is showing. It is evident when he's tired, and he slurs as though his jaw is filled with Novocain.

It really hit home recently when Valerie, Maddie, and I traveled with Mom and Dad to visit relatives in Virginia. Moments before we departed to head back home, I asked my Dad's cousin's wife, Diane, to take a picture of us in her back yard. Mom and I had to walk Dad to the spot where we stood for the picture.

This was something new to see and experience. Dad was wearing his two leg braces at the time, but he had already packed his cane in the trunk of our car for the trip home. As a result, he could not manage the few steps on his own.

This startled me. With his cane or walker, Dad walks relatively fine, under the circumstances. I had seen him without his cane or walker, but he had always been in his house at the time and there had always been something nearby — a chair, a wall — on which he could grab hold and use to help take his next step.

As always, I hid the surprise and discouragement I felt as Dad locked his arms in Mom's and mine and stepped slowly across our relatives' lawn for the picture. Maybe I had been in denial, but I had not known, or accepted, that my father could not walk, period.

I knew he could fall, though, that's for sure. I have seen Dad lose his balance and fall to the ground with an odd grace that plays out in slow motion. There was that time, for example, when he banged his head on the raised lid of my van's trunk and fell flat on his back on the pavement when we visited the University of Maine at Orono during the spring of 2007. I have, however, never witnessed his nastier spills, in which he says he falls back with such force that he bangs the back of his head on the floor of his living room or bathroom.

In 2007, Dad and I attended the ALS Association's national conference in Washington, D.C. We were talking to some acquaintances in the lobby when another ALS patient in a motorized wheelchair accidentally bumped Dad ever so slightly and sent him falling on his rear end. Dad laughed at the incident and claimed not to be embarrassed, but the moment sent pangs through my heart. I did not like seeing Dad knocked down.

That's why I've assumed the role as Dad's "right-hand man." If Dad has to make a few public comments or give a speech at a podium or a standing microphone, I'm always right there behind him, a shy guy in full view of everyone he's addressing. If he shifts to the right, I move left, and vice versa. I always position myself where I think I'd need to be to catch him in case he falls back.

If he's climbing stairs, I'm right behind him. If he's descending them, I am a couple of steps ahead of him. I suppose it'd be smarter if I was right beside him, on the same step, offering my arm to help give him balance and supplement the banister he's using on the other side of him. But then what would break his fall if he tumbled downward?

These are little things, I guess, but they matter greatly to me. Every son or daughter with a terminally ill parent wonders, hopes, and prays they're doing enough to help, to make a difference. Without fail, my father has always been there for me throughout my life. After decades of his love, attention and support, he has given more to me than I ever could do in return for him, especially since the time to try to do so has been cut so short.

At dinner the other night, my friend asked me how Dad is doing, and I told him he's "hanging in there," still on his feet and able to drive and get around and socialize. My friend marveled at the atypically slow progression of Dad's ALS and reiterated what we all once figured, that Dad has perhaps a relatively plentiful ten years still left to live.

I sat up, straightened and leaned back in my booth.

"We don't really think that, anymore," I said, and then added, "I can tell you Dad sure hopes he does not have ten years left."

It's true. He even says it in this book, right? *He welcomes death. He craves its finality.* Those are tough words to see and to hear. My family and I need to accept them. We're not there yet.

ALS has been a part of our lives for four-and-a-half years now. So much has changed. I can remember what Dad looked like when he ran — say, when he hustled across the field during a soccer practice, or chased the bus that had closed its doors on my nine-year-old sister and started pulling away from us in Washington, D.C. — but I've lost all memory of how he once walked. It's ironic, and tragic, because going for long walks with Dad was one of my favorite things to do when I was growing up. We'd take long strolls around town and talk about movies and politics; he'd give me advice about school or help me keep my chin up after a girlfriend and I would part and go our own separate ways.

I can't remember the last walk we took.

Dad has titled this book, "I Prefer to Laugh." I share his philosophy, although I realize I've not offered one humorous remark or anecdote here to provide you the evidence. Not too many people stand by the quotes they put underneath their senior class pictures in their high school yearbooks; after all, years pass and a quote by Van Halen that felt cool and true in 1987 seems embarrassing, dated, and trite in 2009. For my yearbook quote, though, I put, "He who laughs, lasts." I believe that. Dad is proof of it.

My family and I have lived with ALS since 2004. The disease has cut short my father's career, robbed him and my mother of their golden years together, and transformed my warm, old-fashioned childhood home into something handicapped accessible with a long wheelchair ramp on the outside and a new, first-floor bathroom on the inside.

Sometimes, our loved ones are taken without warning, whether by traffic accidents, diagnoses of cancers that are caught too late, or other cruel twists of Fate. ALS usually strikes quickly, stripping its victims of their mobility and independence, and leaving them paralyzed and helpless in a short time. My family and I admittedly are fortunate, if ever the words "fortunate" and "ALS" could be used in the same sentence. Watching Dad's demise is painful and heartbreaking, but we have been given the time to prepare for the inevitable; I have been given the time to remake my mind as it must be remade, become my own man, and enjoy with my father a dear friendship and bond that's becoming purer and less complicated as I make my own mark in the world.

Sometimes I do a mental exercise that's at once wistful and pointless. I try to imagine what life would be like today if Dad did not have ALS. In this alternative reality, Dad is still thriving at work for the University of Maine System and enjoying an active role in shaping community affairs. He walks, laughs, and eats with ease and plots trips with Mom for the years ahead. His mortality never enters his mind; he's in the moment, completely trusting he still has an untold number of years, or decades, ahead of him. Under such a scenario, Mom is happier, more relaxed and assured, confident that her future with Dad is secured with opportunities for getaways and grandchildren.

And me? Well, I wonder.

I wonder if I would have performed more effectively and winningly when I started a new job I accepted before Dad's diagnosis but started just three weeks after it.

I wonder if the purchase of my first home and my return to Sanford after more than eight years out of town would have been more joyful.

I wonder what that first year after Dad's diagnosis would have been like without the sadness, confusion, and despair. It would have been happier for my wife and daughter, that's for sure.

These are normal but unproductive thoughts. Life is filled with setbacks, challenges, and losses. We can't control what happens. We *can* control how we react, adapt, and proceed, though.

Just look at my Dad. Since his diagnosis, he has served as vice-president of a chapter of the ALS Association, lobbied legislators for causes related to the disease, raised funds and awareness for research and a cure, started and presided over a corporation, and written this book.

While these accomplishments stem from his nature — he has always kept busy and come up with new ideas — they nonetheless represent a choice. In December of 2004, Dad could have retreated into his home, shut the door, and waited to die. He could have skipped the waiting and taken the route chosen by his father. Nobody would have blamed him.

Instead, Dad has preferred to laugh. He has chosen to stay active and spend his diminishing energy and ability to helping those who share his fate but may not have the same tools or blessings.

Dad has always been a good man. ALS has made him a great one.

I Prefer to Laugh

CHAPTER 12

TO SIR WITH LOVE
A wife's perspective

By Lorraine C. Sullivan

When my husband asked me to write a chapter for his book, I told him that it would not be all roses, but bittersweet.

I said, "It might show a dark side of ALS. "

"ALS is dark," he replied. "There's no getting around it."

My heart goes out to my husband. As an individual, he alone experiences this disease. I can only give and write my views and interpretations as a spouse. It has been a journey trying to see through his eyes what he is going through day by day.

I am always saddened when I hear that someone has been diagnosed with ALS. It all comes back to me in a flashback of December 8, 2004. It is a mental exercise to remember the unknown of that day and then pull yourself back to the present and live for today.

After the initial shock, you don't see a future for you and your spouse. It has been wiped out. There's no retirement after raising a family and working all your lives. The enjoyment of watching your grandchildren grow up and sharing the joys of holding great grandchildren in your arms has been taken away. Life has played a dirty trick on you, and you didn't see it coming.

It amazes me that I cannot remember the feeling and routine of what life used to be like. Today, we concentrate on ALS. Gary has done so well in dealing with ALS. He never complains. He told me that I think of ALS more than he does. I believe this is true, as I face life with a terminally ill spouse and have to adjust to life afterwards.

Over the years, I have known two individuals whose husbands passed away from pancreatic cancer. One husband lived for six months, and the other lived for three. Each spouse told me that they thought it was harder for me because I live every day with what lies ahead. Each one stated that they eventually had relief because the suffering was for a short term.

A lot of how I feel can be associated somewhat with anyone who has a spouse facing any terminal illness. There are diseases in which we all share a common ground as to how to deal with our lives and our feelings.

Our son, Shawn, commented how he had a hard time remembering how his Dad used to walk. We adjusted to his walking slowly with his cane. I remember watching Gary walk across the street and up the hill. Those types of memories will always stay with me.

Our daughter, Kelly, told me that she experiences the sadness as she drives to work. When I was working, that's when I experienced the sadness too. Both Kelly and I would be fine once we got to work. But you always have that cloud over your head.

One good thought that stays with Gary and me has to do with the October before he was diagnosed. He had a neck operation on several vertebrae. Throughout his recuperation period, we would take long walks under a beautiful blue autumn sky. He was beginning to feel better and was on the road to recovery. We felt that we were on the other side - the healing side. It was a euphoric feeling. It is those days that I reflect upon to recapture that feeling we both felt. It makes me feel good inside to know we did have those glorious days together. It was two months later that he was diagnosed with Lou Gehrig's disease.

We all deal with ALS differently. I remember the disbelief and shock when I heard the news. I can remember telling a friend that I would sell my soul to the devil, if I could, in order that my husband would not have ALS. I recall the stunned look on my friend's face. My statement surprised her, as she had never faced such devastation.

In the process of grieving, I went right to the bargaining stage. How could this have been allowed to happen to such a good man, a man who enjoys life to the fullest? A person who sees the good in everyone and always believes in treating others the way he would like to be treated?

Eventually, we moved on. We focused on the present.

In February of 2005, we took a trip to Florida and spent a couple of days visiting Sanibel Island, where I walked on the beach at sunrise. The sunsets were beautiful.

Our cabin was beneath the coconut-filled palm trees along the shoreline. We gathered seashells and took them home. We bought a special jar from the island to display the shells. They are now in our home, and we get to dream about our stay on the island every time we see them.

On the island, Gary bought a plaque shaped like a sand dollar. It read, *"I am not afraid of tomorrow, for I have seen yesterday...and I love today."* Today, that plaque has a special place in our home.

In August of 2005, we attended a conference on "Research Initiatives and Treatments in ALS" in Portsmouth, New Hampshire. It was an educational conference to explore the research frontier and management of the disease. Our daughter, Kelly, attended the event with us. We attended workshops covering nutritional support, pulmonary issues, speech and swallowing, technology use, and communication systems. For us, this opened the door to what ALS was all about.

In May of 2006, Gary and I went to the ALS Association's conference in Washington, D.C. We weren't sure how we would feel or how we would handle it. We were pleased when everyone we came across with ALS was so upbeat and delighted to be in Washington for this conference.

After the conference, we continued to live our lives as simply and normally as possible. By then, Gary was disabled and retired, but I continued working. We had always said that when we retired we would like to travel throughout our country. After Gary's diagnosis, we decided to take that trip in the fall. During the last two weeks in September and the first two weeks in October of 2005, we took that retirement trip. What a wonderful trip it was to travel 4,400 miles on the open road.

We traveled from Maine to Williamsburg, Virginia, Charleston, South Carolina, and Savannah, Georgia. We then crossed the Great Smoky Mountains to Knoxville, Nashville, and Memphis, Tennessee. Our next destination took us to Branson, Missouri. From that point, we traveled to South Bend, Indiana, visiting Notre Dame University. We then started to head back home, stopping in Cooperstown, New York, to visit the "Baseball Hall of Fame." We saw Lou Gehrig's locker, and his baseball shirt #4. This memorabilia meant more to us than the average person. So much had taken place since Gehrig's July 4, 1939, "The Luckiest Man" speech. We finished our trip at the Norman Rockwell Museum in Stockbridge, Massachusetts. What a wonderful retirement vacation.

In October, 2006, we visited San Antonio, Texas. This part of our retirement trip had to be postponed in 2005 due to Hurricane Katrina.

Over the years, we have had the adventure of traveling to 41 out of the 50 states. We also have traveled to Canada, Mexico, Ireland, England, France, and Italy. Our sense of exploring was always one of our loves in life.

In raising our children, we always took an annual family vacation and, as a result, our children also appreciate the world of travel.

When Gary was diagnosed with ALS in 2004, the process of losing him slowly started with each passing day. I am often reminded with the slight, gradual decline of his health that ALS is definitely a family disease, as it affects and impacts all of us.

It makes me aware that the clock is ticking. When I look at my husband now, I see the same person I met 40 years ago. ALS has not changed his personality. His sense of humor is still intact, even though he has this horrific disease. He is such a crusader when it comes to ALS, demonstrating such determination to accomplish and leave this world a better place, especially for those with ALS.

Over the years, Gary has provided his family with a good life. Every day counts, and we continue to do the best we can. Some days are better than others. We try to see our grandchildren as often as possible and enjoy doing everyday things with them. They bring us tremendous joy.

As for Shawn and Kelly, they have been given a lot to process.

***

Spring is Gary's favorite season. In 2008, he planted a beautiful perennial garden in back of our house. I know that this was planted for me to enjoy with him and in the years to come.

We have been blessed with family, dear and caring classmates, and good and sincere friends. Everyone has been so supportive, and we are grateful to have each of them in our lives.

You're probably wondering how I arrived at the title for my chapter in this book. The movie, "To Sir, With Love," was playing at the Capitol Theater in 1967 when I first met Gary, who was a teacher at the time. He was standing in line in front of me with a classmate friend. From that moment on, we became good friends and started dating a few years later. He is my best friend.

I Prefer to Laugh

EPILOGUE

I'll wait for the movie

The following piece was written by my son, Shawn,
the editor of the Sanford News, a weekly newspaper
in Sanford, Maine. It appeared in his column,
From the Editor's Desk, *on February 12, 2009.*

Who would you have play you in a movie about your life?

It's a frivolous question but a dicey one. If you pick someone glamorous, you risk making those around you laugh at your delusion. If you sell yourself short, then you reveal how you see yourself and for a moment affect how others may as well.

There's a reason. When asked such a question, we more often than not try to pick someone who we think *looks* like us, not someone whose stellar acting talents would do justice to our complexities.

Case in point. My father has written a book. It's called "I Prefer to Laugh," and it's his autobiographical account of living with Lou Gehrig's disease for the past five years. It's an honest account that confronts the horror and sadness of living with ALS but also makes clear the empowerment of choosing humor and advocacy to deal with it. Dad read excerpts from the book to a crowd at Goodall Library last week. He hopes to self-publish his manuscript in time for May, which is National ALS Awareness Month.

I'm editing the book. Kelly, my sister, has little time to read – she's an elementary school teacher and the mother of an energetic toddler – so she has told Dad she's going to skip the book and wait for the movie. Kelly's the one in the family who keeps Dad's feet on the ground.

Kelly's remark prompted speculation when we all met recently for lunch at Newick's in Dover. We started imagining who'd play Dad in the film adaptation of his book.

"Well, first of all, it'd be one of those movies on the Lifetime channel," Kelly offered.

What?" Dad asked. "My life's not good enough to play in theaters?"

"Actually, Lifetime's probably too classy," my brother-in-law, Jay, said. "The USA Network is probably more of the right one."

I just laughed and mocked a broadcaster's voice and said, *"Alan Alda stars as Gary Sullivan in USA Network's movie…"*

I was teasing, of course. Alan Alda's a fine actor, but he fit right for my ribbing because he's always had a rather safe, generic, milquetoast persona, if you ask me.

Alan Alda, however, never crossed Dad's mind. No, he had someone else in mind to play him, should Hollywood ever come knocking. He told us which actor when we all went to The

Olive Garden a couple of nights later. My family likes going out to eat a lot.

"I know who should play me in a movie," Dad said that night. "Matt Damon."

We immediately burst out laughing. Even my five-year-old daughter, Madeline, joined the fun, and she has no idea who Matt Damon is.

Dad feigned wounded offense as families at surrounding tables busted their guts too.

"Matt Damon?" I asked. "Boy, you must think you're something else. You do know People Magazine named him 'Sexiest Man Alive,' right?"

"Yeah, but he's a good actor," Dad replied.

"He is, Dad, but he's 30 years younger than you."

"Well, I'm talking about who should play me when I was young," he countered.

"You're more like John Cleese," my wife, Valerie, offered. "You have the same build."

We all tried to picture it. I had never considered John Cleese, the British comedian from "Monty Python" and "A Fish Called Wanda," to be my father's doppelganger. Nah. When I was a kid I thought Dad looked a bit like Chevy Chase.

Dad grimaced at Valerie's mention of Cleese's name. Cleese is funny but no one's idea of appealing, he figured.

"Actually, Dad, coming from Valerie, that's a compliment," I told him.

It's true. Valerie's type is tall and skinny men. And if they speak with an English accent and look and sound like they belong in a Jane Austen novel, then all the better for her. It's always been a curious and hilarious fact of our marriage that *I'm* not even Valerie's type.

Dad wasn't buying. He was still pushing for Damon. Cleese was out.

My mother had her own suggestion. Walter Matthau.

"Mom, he's dead," I told her.

She thought about that for a moment, and then said it didn't matter. Matthau would be the right guy to play Dad.

"So you're saying I look like a dead guy from the 'Grumpy Old Men' movies?" Dad asked.

Mom didn't say anything. She just shrugged her shoulders, as though to say, "If the shoe fits…"

But then Mom had her own idea about who should play her in a movie: Angela Lansbury. At this point I could see Mom's version of Dad's movie in my head. It's not anything I'd pay to see. Or watch for free on USA Network.

Valerie and I both agreed she'd be played by the actress Julie Haggerty, from those "Airplane" comedies from the early eighties. She sort of looks like Haggerty and definitely sounds like her.

Me? I stayed out of it. I did not cast the role of me in Dad's movie daydream. I have a good sense of humor about myself, but that doesn't mean I go around setting myself up to be told I'm no George Clooney.

I do get told once in a while that I look like so-and-so or so-and-so. Sometimes it's flattering. Other times I walk away and shake my head and ask, *"Now why would someone say that?"*

I suppose if they did make a movie out of Dad's book, then there's at least one guy who could play him as a younger man.

Me.

I get told I look like my father all the time.

Wait a minute.

Does this mean I look like Walter Matthau?

I Prefer to Laugh

SECTION III

ONE DISEASE

Dedicated to

Mukesh Bhargava M.D.
Primary Care Physician

Lisa Krivickas M.D.
Physiatrist/Neuromuscular Medicine Specialist

I would like to express my deepest appreciation to

Drs. Bhargava and Krivickas

for their tremendous support and understanding throughout my journey with Lou Gehrig's disease (ALS).

Their professionalism, compassion, and acceptance of my sense of humor have enabled me to survive the past five years with dignity and knowledge.

Section III provides an insight into the progression of my Amyotrophic Lateral Sclerosis (ALS) through a series of medical benchmarks and a chronology of health reports. Some notes have been edited, especially in areas where no medical changes had occurred.

WARNING! By the very nature of medical notes, one can get lost in their terminology and the tediousness of the reporting. Normally, this section would be inserted as an appendix but its importance warrants it being part of the story's main body of work.

126

INTRODUCTION

Amyotrophic Lateral Sclerosis

by Diane Sullivan

Many times when people hear the words "Amyotrophic Lateral Sclerosis," they do not necessarily think of the disease that is better known as "ALS" or "Lou Gehrig's disease," unless they are familiar with someone they know who has had it. This is an attempt to present some factual information from various sources in helping the reader to understand ALS, which was identified in 1869 by the French neurologist Jean-Martin Charcot.

In simple terms, the *World Book Encyclopedia* defines ALS as "a rare, incurable disease of the nervous system." No race or social or economic class is sacred, and "it afflicts almost twice as many men as women."[1]

The ALS Association's (ALSA) website defines ALS as a "progressive neurodegenerative disease that affects nerve cells in the brain and the spinal cord. Motor neurons reach from the brain to the spinal cord and from the spinal cord to the muscles throughout the body. The progressive degeneration of the motor neurons in ALS eventually leads to their death. When the motor neurons die, the ability of the brain to initiate and control muscle movement is lost. With voluntary muscle action progressively affected, patients in the later stages of the disease may become totally paralyzed."[2] When motor neurons cannot send impulses to the muscle fibers that cause the muscles to move, there is muscle weakness, especially in the arms and legs, speech, swallowing, or breathing. When the muscles do not receive the impulses from the motor neurons, the muscles begin to atrophy. Consequently, "the limbs become thinner as the muscle tissue atrophies. The patients lose their strength and the ability to move their arms, legs, and body. When muscles in the diaphragm and chest wall fail, patients lose the ability to breathe without ventilatory support."[2] According to the National Institute of Health, most people with ALS die from respiratory failure, usually within three to five years from the onset of symptoms. However, about ten percent of ALS patients survive for ten or more years.[3]

ALSA's website explains the word "a-myo-trophic," uniquely by showing its Greek origin. "*A* means no or negative. *Myo* refers to muscle, *trophic* means nourishment – *no muscle nourishment.*" Without nourishment, the muscle atrophies. *Lateral* identifies the areas in a person's spinal cord where portions of the nerve cells that signal and control the muscles are located. As this area degenerates, it leads to scarring or hardening (*sclerosis*) in the region."[2]

Although the disease usually does not impair a person's mind or intelligence, several recent studies suggest that some ALS patients may have alterations in cognitive functions such as depression and problems with decision-making and memory. ALS does not affect a person's ability to see, smell, taste, hear, or recognize touch. Individuals usually maintain control of eye muscles and bladder and bowel functions; however, they will need help with their mobility.[3]

According to the ALSA and several other sources, "approximately 5,600 people in the U.S. are diagnosed with ALS each year. The incidence of ALS is two per 100,000 people, and it is estimated that as many as 30,000 Americans may have the disease at any given time."[2] ALS is not contagious, and it is one of the most common neuromuscular diseases in the world. In 90 to 95 percent of all ALS cases, the disease seems to occur at random with no clearly associated risk factors. Patients do not have a family history of the disease, and their family members are not considered to be at increased risk for developing ALS. About five to ten percent of all ALS cases are inherited.

The onset of ALS may be so subtle that the symptoms are frequently overlooked. The earliest symptoms may include twitching, cramping, or stiffness of muscles; muscle weakness affecting an arm or a leg; slurred and nasal speech; or difficulty chewing or swallowing. These general complaints then develop into more obvious weakness or atrophy that may cause a physician to suspect ALS. The parts of the body affected by early symptoms of ALS depend on which muscles in the body are damaged first. In some cases, symptoms initially affect one of the legs, and patients experience awkwardness when walking or running, or they notice that they are tripping or stumbling more often. Some patients first see the effects of the disease on a hand or arm as they experience difficulty with simple tasks requiring manual dexterity such as buttoning a shirt, writing, or turning a key in a lock. Other patients notice speech problems.[2]

For an ALS diagnosis, patients must have the signs and symptoms of both upper and lower motor neuron damage that cannot be attributed to other causes. According to the ALS Therapy Development Institute, "ALS is diagnosed using a variety of tests and examinations, including laboratory tests, muscle and nerve biopsies, spinal tap, X-rays, MRIs and electrodiagnostic tests."[4] No one test can provide a definitive diagnosis of ALS, although the presence of upper and lower motor neuron signs in a single limb is strongly suggestive. Instead, the diagnosis of ALS is primarily based on the symptoms and signs the physician observes in the patient and a series of tests to rule out other diseases. Physicians obtain the patient's full medical history and usually conduct a neurologic examination at regular intervals to assess whether symptoms such as muscle weakness, atrophy of muscles, hyperreflexia, and spasticity are getting progressively worse.

The National Institute of Neurological Disorders and Stroke, part of the National Institutes of Health, is the federal government's leading supporter of biomedical research on ALS. The goals of this research are to find the cause or causes of ALS, understand the mechanisms involved in the progression of the disease, and develop effective treatment.[3]

ALS is not completely understood, and scientists have not been able to determine what causes the motor neurons to degenerate and die, but in the more recent years, there has been a wealth of new scientific understanding about the physiology of ALS.[2]

The Robert Packard Center for ALS Research at Johns Hopkins has made great strides in creating new animal models of ALS along with the introduction of astrocytes grown from human stem cells. Stem cell and gene therapy research, which may show promising results, continues at the Packard Center.[5]

References

1   "Amyotrophic lateral sclerosis." *The World Book Encyclopedia*. page 450, 1988 ed.
2   www.alsa.org/als

3   www.ninds.nih.gov/disorders/amyotrophiclateralscl
      erosis/detail_amyotrophiclateralsclerosis.htm
4   www.als.net/als101/whatisals.asp
5   Robert Packard Center at Johns Hopkins. 2008
      Annual Report.
      www.alscenter.org/annualreport2008/ALS_Annual_
      Report_2008.pdf

I Prefer to Laugh

CHAPTER 13

GARY'S ANATOMY

In order to monitor the progression of my ALS it is necessary to establish a medical baseline at a time prior to the onset of my disease.

My primary care physician is Dr. Mukesh Bhargava. He moved to Sanford, Maine, in the summer of 2001.

On October 17, 2001, I had my first appointment with Dr. Bhargava and his medical notes serve as a baseline from which to compare future medical events.

Primary Care Physician - Office Notes – 10/17/2001

<u>Chief Complaint:</u> 1. Establish primary care 2. Neck pain

<u>History of Presenting Illness:</u> 56-year-old man with hyper-cholesterolemia, hypertension, and arthritis at the neck comes in today to establish primary care. He had been doing work on his house and this activated his neck pain. He has done some exercises that were prescribed to him last year with moderate

relief. He does not complain of any weakness or sensory symptoms in his arm.

<u>Review of System:</u>

<u>Family History:</u> Dad committed suicide; sister had brain tumor

<u>Diagnosis:</u> Hypercholesterolemia, Benign Hypertension

<u>Physical Exam:</u> Height 71 inches, BP 130/80mm/hg, Weight 180 pounds, PR 78/m

Neck: Supple no thyromegaly or lymphadenopathy.

Heart: Normal intensity heart sounds with no added sounds. No gallops, rubs or murmurs.

Lungs: Good air entry on both sides. No added sounds. No stridor.

Extremities: No edema cyanosis or clubbing. Pulses equal on both sides.

Neurological: Alert-oriented to time place and person. No focal deficits.

Assessment	Medical Reasoning and Plan
Hypertension	Well-controlled, continue present medication
Hypercholesterolemia	Well-controlled, check lipid profile in April
Neck pain	Arthritis, no evidence of radiculopathy

***

In January 2002, I visited a neurologist to assess pain I was having in my neck, shoulders and right arm.

Neurologist notes – 01/29/2002

<u>History:</u> This patient is a 56-year-old right-handed gentleman who states that two years ago he did some heavy work cleaning windows. At that time, he developed severe pain in his neck and across both shoulders and along with that he had pain extending down his right arm. He doesn't remember numbness in the right hand or arm. He saw an orthopedic assistant, had X-rays, MRI scan, and cervical disc disease was documented. He underwent a few months of physical therapy. He was recovered completely in three months' time.

He states that more recently, in October 2001, he had three projects requiring heavy computer work. During that time, he developed pain in two areas; one was an extensor surface of his right forearm extending into his hand with occasional paresthesias in the right fifth digit. He also developed pain in the right area near the scapula. This would extend up and down the spine and both sides and was quite severe at times. He went on Vioxx for that and has been off that treatment for the last two weeks. The problem has improved dramatically. He also has received physical therapy to his neck and right arm and with stretching exercises along with the ergonomic changes at work he was feeling much better. He came in for a baseline testing.

<u>Physical examination:</u> Motor bulk strength normal, tone normal, reflexes 2+ throughout with 1+ right triceps jerk. Sensory examination was normal to primary modalities. He had a negative Phalen's sign bilaterally. Tinel's sign at the ulnar groove was negative bilaterally and Spurling's maneuver to the right was normal.

<u>Electrophysiologic Testing:</u> Motor conduction studies, and F wave latencies were normal. Electromyography (EMG) sampling right upper extremity was within normal limits. *(EMG*

measures the electrical impulses of muscles at rest and during contraction.)

<u>Electrophysiologic Impression:</u> Within normal limits.

<u>Clinical Impression:</u> The spell two years ago sounds as though it may have been a cervical radiculopathy[1]. I say that because he had documented cervical disc disease on his MRI scan and he has a depressed right triceps jerk. Although the symptom complex is a little hard to sort out; in retrospect, I suspect that accounts for his symptoms at that point in time. This current bout occurred after heavy use with a computer. His right forearm and hand symptoms sound more like extensor tendonitis, perhaps some nerve irritation. In addition, he has pain across his shoulder blades. On this occasion I didn't find a very clear history for radiculopathy and certainly couldn't find anything on clinical exam or EMG to support that. In addition, EMG sampling did not document a significant compression neuropathy.

***

Parasite and Potential Effects?

While on vacation in the summer of 2002, I contracted a parasite that resulted in diarrhea for a run of 19 days. It is unlikely that this medical episode had any bearing on the onset of my disease, but due to ALS's unknown cause it is included here to provide a thorough medical history.

---

[1] Radiculopathy: Any disease of the spinal nerve roots and spinal nerves.

Primary Care Physician - Phone Call - 06/26/2002

<u>Subjective:</u> Diarrhea for four days without associated bleeding, abdominal pain or fever.

<u>Assessment:</u> Viral gastroenteritis

<u>Plan:</u> Oral hydration, warning signs discussed. Patient is in New Jersey

Primary Care Physician - Phone Call - 7/01/2002

Diarrhea - nine days

<u>Lab Report:</u> Parasites found are as follows: Entamoeba Coli Rare Trophs

***

First Symptoms or Coincidence?

In the fall of 2002 I began to develop muscle cramps and swallowing issues.

Primary Care Physician - Progress Notes - 12/02/2002

Occasionally, Mr. Sullivan has noticed that he is conscious of swallowing; this does not happen with any specific foods or at any specific times. He has also noticed some muscle cramps, which have decreased with increasing his water intake. Weight 176 pounds.

Assessment	Medical Reasoning and Plan
Difficulty swallowing	Unlikely to be related to structural Disease. Conduct barium swallow to exclude intraluminal abnormalities.
Muscle cramps	Recommend increase ectrolyte intake.

Diagnostic Imaging - Radiology Result - 12/09/2002

Procedure Reason: Dysphagia[2]

Findings: The patient was able to swallow barium and air without difficulty. There is a very small reducible hiatal hernia. The esophagus shows no obvious focal abnormality but there is noted to be a trace amount of gastroesophageal reflux with provocative maneuvers. The stomach, duodenal bulb, C sweep, and proximal portions of the small bowel are unremarkable.

Impression: Small hernia and trace amount of gastroesophageal reflux as described.

---

[2] Dysarthria: a disorder caused by paralysis, weakness, or inability to coordinate the muscles of the mouth.

CHAPTER 14

THE ONSET

It was June 14, 2003 – my fifty-ninth birthday. To celebrate, Lorraine treated me to dinner at a Cajun restaurant in New Hampshire. The bar did not make margaritas, my favorite drink, so I settled for one made with rum.

I thought it best to order something safe, so I settled on scallops. The meal came with potatoes and vegetables.

The whole meal was fiery hot and could not have burned more if they served it flaming. I had never tasted spicy scallops before. Washing it down with rum was like throwing fuel on a fire.

I do not eat hot or spicy foods because they irritate my stomach, so one would wonder why my wife chose THAT restaurant for my birthday. But that's a tale for another day.

After the meal from "hell," I returned home to attend a local baseball game. I got a hot dog, soda, and a bag of popcorn.

After the game, I was home watching television and finishing up a piece of my cake when my daughter called to wish me happy birthday.

As we talked I began to cough, then choke, and gasp for air.

I set the phone down on the table. I stood in the kitchen, trying to catch my breath, leaving the line open, making it impossible for my daughter to call for help. She was left listening to her Dad choke, and there was nothing she could do.

My wife, who had been asleep upstairs, heard the noise and thought that our cat, O'Rourke, was coughing up a fur ball. She soon realized that was not the case and ran down the stairs to see if I was OK.

Gradually, I began to take in some air.

I felt that I was going to die on that Saturday night, six years ago.

I had suffered similar, smaller attacks weeks earlier, but they were nothing like that evening's episode.

That Monday I called my physician.

Primary Care Physician - Phone Call - 06/16/2003

Episode Saturday Night (06/14/2003) couldn't breathe – lasted for 1.5 to 2 minutes. Has had these episodes 3 or 4 times before for much shorter periods of time. Notices heavier breathing at night.

Primary Care Physician - Progress Notes - 06/17/2003

<u>Assessment</u>: Gastroesophageal Reflux Disease (GERD)

<u>Plan</u>: Start Prilosec 40mg.

Primary Care Physician - Progress Notes - 11/13/03

Gary has had episodic choking when he has had too much to eat. This is associated with significant reflux. He has had an upper GI endoscopy that showed hiatal hernia. No other structural lesions were found. We discussed the use of medications like Reglan to prevent this. The dilemma is that his symptoms are only once every three to four months but are fairly scary and he would be taking the medicine for no significant indication in the interim. However, he is concerned enough that he would like to try it. He also describes muscle aches that start in his legs but then spread to the rest of the body. He is concerned about muscle toxicity of statins. These pains are described as in certain positions; they are not true myalgias. I would still plan on checking CK and holding off on Lipitor.

Blood Work: Creatinine kinase (CK) 380 (high) Reference range 35-232

Primary Care Physician - Progress Notes - 12/12/2003

Fifty-eight-year-old otherwise healthy gentleman presents to the office for repeated choking spells. These have been precipitated by food; sometimes popcorn. He has not lost consciousness. He was started on proton pump inhibitors and Reglan without significant change. He had also described some muscle aches which were associated with elevated CK. Lipitor *(a statin used for the control of cholesterol)* was discontinued and muscle aches have markedly improved.

Assessment	Medical Reasoning and Plan
Choking spells	Differential diagnosis includes active medical abnormalities, muscle dysfunction, global hystericus. I would plan on rechecking CK, serum calcium, speech and swallowing consultation, chest x-ray, discontinue Ace inhibitors and start angiotensin receptor blockers.

Diagnostic Imaging - Radiology Results - 12/15/2003

Procedure: RAD/ Swallowing study, video Fluoro

Reason: Cough, difficulty swallowing

Findings: Modified video swallowing study was performed in conjunction with speech therapy. The patient drank varying consistencies of liquid barium as well as swallowing varying consistencies of solid food mixed with barium. There are no abnormalities to swallowing function. No aspiration or penetration occurs during this study. There is no evidence for pooling. There is no Zenker's diverticulum. The patient swallows a 12-mm barium tablet. This passes somewhat slowly through the thoracic esophagus suggesting there may be slight diminished esophageal motility. However, there are no obstructing lesions. There is no hiatal hernia.

Impression: Slightly diminished esophageal motility; otherwise, no structural abnormalities or swallowing dysfunction. CK 258

***

The ALS Connection *webpage explains the effects of acid reflux and laryngospasms and their relationships to ALS.*

Acid Reflux

Acid reflux, also known as gastroesophageal reflux disease (GERD), is a common condition in people with ALS. It is due to weakness of the diaphragm muscles involved in breathing, which normally form a tight band around the opening to the stomach to keep the acids down. The signs and symptoms may include heartburn, acid taste, throat irritation, chest pain, hoarseness, shortness of breath, nausea, insomnia, and even spasms of the larynx. These symptoms are thought to be caused by the reflux of stomach acid into the lower esophagus. Caffeine, spicy foods, overeating, and diaphragm weakness all increase acid reflux into the esophagus.

Laryngospasm (Tightening of the Throat)

Laryngospasm is an abrupt and prolonged closure of the vocal cords, resulting in sudden gasping for breath and wheezing. This can cause panic because of the fear of suffocation. Laryngospasm may also occur with increased emotion or with exposure to smoke, strong smells, alcohol, cold or rapid bursts of air, and even spicy foods. It can also occur with sinus or postnasal drip, as well as acid reflux.

Laryngospasm normally clears spontaneously in a few seconds, but can be more immediately relieved by breathing through the nose and repetitively swallowing. Possible triggers of laryngospasm should be eliminated and a trial of antacids instituted. Understanding the nature of this process can usually help to calm the panic that aggravates laryngospasm.[3]

---

[3] http://www.alsconnection.com/ "Treating the Symptoms" pp 96-7

When I visited Dr. Lisa Krivickas at Massachusetts General Hospital (MGH) in January of 2005, for a second opinion on my Lou Gehrig's diagnosis, she told Lorraine and me that she believed the onset of my ALS was 18 months earlier. Which brings us back to that night in June 2003?

I Prefer to Laugh

One Man, One Family, One Disease

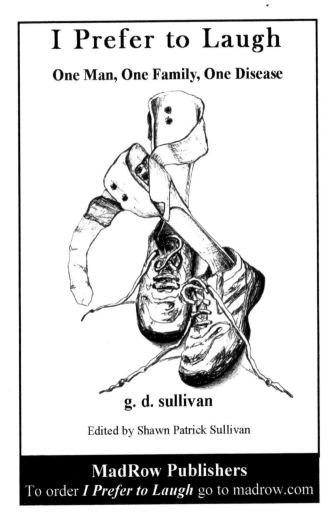

g. d. sullivan

Edited by Shawn Patrick Sullivan

MadRow Publishers
To order *I Prefer to Laugh* go to madrow.com

*"My neurologist's diagnosis
cut through my heart
and pierced my soul,
'You have Lou Gehrig's disease.'*

*Never again would I view
dreams with anticipation,
or retirement with excitement.
The dreams became nightmares;
retirement, a disability.*

That is where the end of my story begins."

g. d. sullivan
I Prefer to Laugh

MadRow Publishers
madrow.com

CHAPTER 15

THE DIAGNOSIS

The pivotal year in my journey with ALS came in 2004. Lou Gehrig's disease is difficult to diagnose, as is evident in the medical notes that follow.

Primary Care Physician - Progress Notes - 1/12/2004

Follow-up of coughing and choking spells. Gary has done well. His choking spells have almost resolved and his cough has also decreased. He saw an Ear, Nose and Throat (ENT) physician who confirmed that his symptoms were related to reflux. We had also discontinued his Lipitor and ACE inhibitor because of cough and myalgias[4]. His CK has come down but not to normal. He feels significantly better. The aches and pains are also better.

Assessment	Medical Reasoning and Plan
Complications of statin medication.	Refrain from statin use.

---

[4] Myalgia: Pain in a muscle

Primary Care Physician - Progress Notes - 3/01/2004

Muscle aches have been completely resolved - no other complaints. He is gradually but definitely feeling much better since he has been discontinued on the statins.

Neurologist - Medical Report - 05/10/2004

Chief Complaint: Myositis[5]

History: Gary relates a one-month history of migratory muscle cramps in the upper and lower extremities and in his flanks. Through the summer and fall *(2003),* he felt a loss of strength and energy in the legs with difficulty climbing the hill from his house to church. He had been on Lipitor for four years. This was discontinued in the fall due to elevated CK. Since then, his muscle cramps have declined and his leg strength has improved. He has noted some weakness of the right foot with a tendency for it to flop when he walks longer distances. This has improved, but not resolved.

His serial CK measurements are 380 last November, 258 in December, 215 in February, and 233 and 258 in April. He has had no pain in the back or pain radiating to either leg. He has had no sensory symptoms.

Review of Systems: There have been three episodes of coughing leading to laryngeal stridor[6], which resolves over several minutes. This was thought to be due to reflux.

Past Medical History: He saw a neurologist in January of 2002, following episodes of upper extremity pain, thought to be cervical radiculopathy in origin. Upper extremity nerve conduction studies were normal.

---

[5] Myositis: Inflammation of muscle tissue.

[6] Stridor: high-pitched breathing sounds due to airway obstruction

Physical Examination: Comprehensive neurologic exam was completed. There is full range of motion of the lumbar spine. Straight leg-raising is negative. Motor exam shows no muscle atrophy[7]. Strength is normal in the upper extremities and left lower extremity. There is 4/5 weakness of dorsiflexion and eversion of the right foot with normal plantar flexion and inversion. Reflexes are 3+ throughout. There is some spread from reflexes from one leg to the other, but no clonus or increased tone. There is a touch of cogwheel rigidity at the elbows. Gait is normal.

Electrical Studies: The right peroneal nerve shows significant slowing between ankle and below the fibular head, normal across the fibular head. The amplitude of the muscle action potential is markedly reduced. There is mild slowing of motor conduction in the right tibial nerve.

EMG shows evidence of acute denervation[8] in the right anterior tibial muscle with prominent positive sharp waves. There are only one or two voluntary motor units. The right EHL and peroneus longus show no spontaneous activity, but only one or two voluntary motor units of normal amplitude. The right gluteus medius shows no spontaneous activity and moderate drop out of voluntary motor units.

Assessment: Elevated CK and cramps: the constellation of muscle cramps, elevated CK, and symptoms of weakness strongly suggest Lipitor-related myositis. Lipitor appropriately was discontinued and CPK and symptoms have improved

---

[7] Atrophy: Wasting away or diminution. Muscle atrophy is wasting of muscle, decrease in muscle mass.

[8] Denervation: Loss of nerve supply. It may be due to a disease where the death of motor neurons causes the denervation of muscle fibers.

significantly. His current examination shows no proximal weakness and EMG shows no evidence of proximal myopathy.

<u>Plan:</u> He should remain off statins long-term if possible.

<u>Assessment:</u> Weakness and denervation changes in a right peroneal distribution. The most common cause is crossing the legs. The patient has lost 10-15 pounds, and this may be a contributory factor to losing some protective padding. His conduction studies show slowing below the fibular head. It is likely that the compression is occurring just below the fibular head. If the nerve injury is not mechanical in etiology, then we must raise the question of mononeuropathy[9] due to another cause. Lumbar radiculopathy is possible, particularly since there is some drop out of uniys in the gluteus medius muscle. However, there is no denervation in other L5-innervated muscles, and there is no history of back pain or pain radiation to the leg.

<u>Plan:</u> I have advised him to stop crossing the legs, particularly the right over the left. No further tests are planned at present.

Neurologist Re-evaluation - 07/13/2004

1. Since May – progressive improvement in energy - only occasional muscle cramps.
2. Right peroneal palsy – improving right lower leg strength – able to walk recently with no "flopping" of the foot. Has avoided crossing the legs.
3. Right cervical radiculopathy – recent flare-up with activities.

<u>Assessment/Plan</u>
1. Lipitor myositis – resolved

---

[9] Mononeuropathy: A disorder of a single nerve or nerve trunk.

2. C 7 radiculopathy – plan, cervical collar at night. Avoid neck extension.
3. Peroneal palsy – presumably with crossing the legs – improving.

Problems with my right arm and thumb further complicated the diagnosis.

Primary Care Physician - Progress Notes - 7/27/2004

Patient complained of neck pain. This has been associated with numbness, tingling, and weakness in the right arm. He was started on narcotics by the neurologist for this suspecting radiculopathy. Symptoms have slightly worsened, and he is not able to have a good night's sleep.

Primary Care Physician - Phone Record - 08/12/2004

Reason: pinched nerve; took last steroid; still bothering him. Plan: arrange MRI of cervical spine.

Radiology Results - 08/17/2004

At the C7-T1 level, marked right foraminal narrowing is seen secondary to prominent right-sided spurring and bulging disc.

Primary Care Physician - Progress Notes - 8/24/2004

Gary had magnetic resonance imaging of the cervical spine; these are consistent with cervical radiculopathy. We agreed to have him see the surgeon and the neurologist to get their opinions as to further management.

Neurologist – Medical Report – 09/01/2004

Mr. Sullivan returns for follow up of a problem which was only touched on in the past. In early July, he over exerted himself and began experiencing recurrence of his right arm radiculopathy. He has had variable pain in the right scapular area, radiating down the arm, and significant weakness of finger extensors, particularly the thumb, which has impaired function.

Examination: Examination shows positive foramen compression maneuver to the right. This produces radicular paresthesias[10] down the right arm.

Ancillary Data: He has advance long-standing chronic partial denervation changes in the right C8 distribution with only a single surviving unit in thumb and finger extensors and a moderately reduced pattern in triceps and flexor digitorum V. There are fibrillations[11] in the extensor muscles of the forearm.

Assessment: Mr. Sullivan's examination, MRI, and electrical studies all indicate chronic right C8 radiculopathy with superimposed acute changes. He has had four or five episodes of radiculopathy over the past few years. His MRI shows a bony bar at right C7-T1.

Plan: He is a good candidate for surgery, considering his recurrent symptoms, chronic denervation changes and the level of weakness. Prognosis for recovery of strength is uncertain.

Surgeon's Pre-Op Report - 09/29/2004

Mr. Sullivan has a significant C8 radiculopathy in the way of motor weakness, though his pain is better. Considering the dysfunction of his dominant hand, I favor proceeding with surgery to enhance his further recovery and hopefully avoid a further neurologic downturn.

---

[10] Paresthesias: abnormal sensations such as burning or prickling

[11] Fibrillation: incoordinate twitching of the muscle fibers

<u>Evaluation</u>: Patient relates a history of five years ago having an episode of right arm pain. He describes a C8 distribution. The patient was treated and things improved with physical therapy. He has had three other episodes. On July 11, 2004, after lifting, the patient developed right C8 pain associated with tingling in all the fingers. He got a little bit of tingling in the fingers of his left side. He also had a feeling of numbness in the right C8 distribution. He then developed scapular area pain and neck pain. He states the hand felt weak and that has continued, including thumb extensor weakness. He noted some slight difficulty walking. He developed some balance problems and started dragging his right foot. The patient has had three sessions of physical therapy in the intervening years and none have been particularly helpful. His current symptomatology is pain in the right C8 distribution associated with paresthesias in the same area. He continues to have thumb and hand weakness. He has occasional incoordination.

<u>Past Medical History:</u> The patient has had myalgia secondary to Lipitor. The patient also has a peroneal palsy on the right as diagnosed by his neurologist. He gets some occasional leg stiffness with ambulation.

Allergies: Lipitor has caused a myalgia syndrome.

Review of Systems: Problems as noted above plus some occasional difficulty swallowing.

<u>Examination:</u> The patient is unable to stand on his heels but can stand on his toes. Cervical spine range of motion is approximately 80% of normal. He has decreased sharp-dull sensation in the ulner distribution on the left and mildly on the median distribution on the right. The patient has 2/5 thumb extensor function on the right. His intrinsic is slightly weak. Finger extensors are slightly weak. Otherwise, strength is intact except for right supinator. Right supinator is minimally weak.

<u>Imaging studies:</u> Imaging studies show C7-T1 disk osteophyte complex with foraminal encroachment on the right. The patient also has other levels with mild stenosis[12] and mild bulging disk but no obvious neurologic compromise.

<u>Plan:</u> Discussed with the patient his condition in detail and treatment alternatives, including surgery and the patient's risks and benefits of surgery. The patient did accept surgery, and this will be booked. Surgical consent was signed today.

***

Post-Op

After my spinal operation, on October 14, there were no plans for me to return to my neurologist, as he determined that my condition did not warrant it. However, at a follow-up with my surgeon, I raised the issue of my dropped foot in an attempt to get some sort of answer. What follows are the written exchanges between my surgeon and the neurologist.

Surgeon's Report to Neurologist - 11/17/2004

I saw Mr. Sullivan back in the office approximately a month after his C8. He reports improvement of his paresthesias and numbness and feels that his strength is improving. His thumb is not better yet. His wound is healing nicely, and he is not on any pain medication. Another concern he raised was discomfort in both distal lower extremities that occurs with walking. This does not have features of vascular claudication, but occurs fairly

---

[12] Stenosis: Narrowing of the spaces in the spine, resulting in compression of the nerve roots or spinal cord by bony spurs or soft tissues, such as disks, in the spinal canal.

regularly with minimal activity and worsens as he continues to stay active. He has had a known statin myopathy, was treated with steroids, and has had a peroneal neuropathy[13]. He has been off the statins for a year and off the steroids for a couple of months. He notes that there has been increasing atrophy of his legs. I think he would greatly appreciate re-evaluation and probably repeat electrodiagnositics of his lower extremities to rule out any other source of progressive weakness, pain, and atrophy. Some other underlying muscle disease seems unlikely, but it is conceivable that we have been misled by the more common statin-related problems.

Neurologist Report to Surgeon - 12/06/2004

History: The patient has continued to have progressive weakness in the lower extremities since I saw him in the summer. His right foot drop has worsened. He now has weakness of the left ankle. The longer he walks, the more the legs tire, to the point where they "won't function." They will progressively slap and he becomes unsteady. After a long walk in Boston, he was unable to get up from a kneeling position. He has had no loss of strength or function in the upper extremities, except for his right thumb. He has no current pain in the neck and no radicular pain to the legs. He has no sensory symptoms, except in the ulnar aspect of the right hand. There are no problems with speech, chewing, or swallowing.

Physical Examination: Comprehensive neurologic exam was completed. Pertinent findings include the following. Cranial nerves are normal. There is no dysarthria. No atrophy of the tongue.

---

[13] Neuropathy: Any and all disease or malfunction of the nerves.

Motor exam: There is some extension of contraction from one leg to the other, but no increased tone or clonus. Gait shows a steppage gait. There is mild instability with feet together.

Electrical Studies: Electrical studies show absent conduction in the right peroneal nerve to the foot. The left peroneal nerve shows markedly reduced amplitude in the muscle action potential with normal motor conduction velocity. EMG shows prominent fasciculations in right anterior tibial, EDB. The EDB shows trains of high- frequency motor unit discharges. There are positive sharp waves in the gastrocnemius. There is no spontaneous activity in the left lower extremity. Voluntary patterns show evidence of chronic partial denervation changes involving all muscles in the right lower extremity, including quadriceps, gluteus medius, anterior tibial, EDB, peroneus. There are mild chronic partial denervation changes in the same muscles in the left lower extremity. EMG in the left upper extremely shows fibrillations in the extensor pollicis longus and first dorsal interosseous. Voluntary patterns are moderately reduced in these muscles. The infroaspinatus shows no spontaneous activity and mildly reduced pattern.

Assessment: Mr. Sullivan has shown progressive weakness, now involving both lower extremities since last seen in summer. His EMG documents a lower motor neuron pattern. His conduction studies are consistent with his motor nerve loss and there is no evidence of significant sensory motor neuropathy. In addition, his examination and electrical studies show some denervation changes in the left upper extremity. In correlation with the very active reflexes and lower motor neuron involvement of all four extremities, a diagnosis of motor neuron disease seems most likely. His lower extremity symptoms could be explained by cauda equine lesion, though the absence of pain makes this very unlikely. He has no bulbar involvement.

<u>Plan:</u> Appropriate blood studies, including heavy metal screen, protein electrophoresis, and motor neuropathy panel. Lumbar MRI scan. Follow-up after studies.

Neurologist's Follow-up to Surgeon - 12/8/2004

Mr. Sullivan's history of progressive lower motor neuron deficits involving both lower extremities and the left upper extremity indicate a near certain diagnosis of motor neuron disease, in my opinion. I reviewed his lumbar spine MRI today, and this does not show evidence of nerve root or cauda equine compression to explain his progressive lower extremity symptoms. His nerve conduction studies do not indicate multifocal motor neuropathy. Still pending are his blood studies, including motor neuropathy antibodies.

The diagnosis was discussed with the patient and his wife. Relatively favorable findings for prognosis include the fact that there are no definite upper motor neuron findings, except possibly mild hyperreflexia[14], and the lack of bulbar involvement or respiratory symptoms. He has had demonstrable, but not marked, progression in six months of my observation.

<u>Plan:</u>
1. Arrange for a second opinion in Boston
2. Begin Rilutek, 50 mg bid.
3. Obtain baseline pulmonary function studies.
4. Follow-up will be planned in six weeks.

Primary Care Physician - Progress Notes - 12/10/2004

Gary comes in fairly depressed, sad, and anxious with his new diagnosis of ALS. He was told by the neurologist yesterday.

---

[14] Hyperreflexia: overactive neurological reflexes

The neurologist has set him up with a second opinion/ consultation in Boston. We talked at length about how to deal with this situation both emotionally and with his family.

<u>Assessment:</u> Possible ALS

Pulmonary Function Study - 12/16/2004

The flow volume loop shows slightly decreased flows and very low lung volumes and otherwise appears normal. The forced vital capacity (FVC) was 83.41 of predicted. Lung volume determination shows normal total lung capacity with minimal reductions in FRC and RV.

CHAPTER 16

POST-DIAGNOSIS

Second Opinion

On January 18, 2005, Lorraine and I traveled to Boston, Massachusetts, for an appointment with Dr. Lisa Krivickas, an ALS specialist at Massachusetts General Hospital (MGH), for a second opinion on my diagnosis. This report will serve as a baseline for monitoring the progression of my ALS.

ALS Specialist - **01/18/2005**

<u>Chief Complaint:</u> Second opinion concerning diagnosis of ALS.

<u>History of Present Illness:</u> Mr. Sullivan is a 59-year-old gentleman who is referred by his primary care physician for a second opinion concerning recent diagnosis of ALS. Mr. Sullivan tells me that he was in his usual state of good health until approximately a year and a half ago, when he seemed to develop generalized muscle weakness. At that time, he was taking Lipitor and was found to have a serum CK of 350. The Lipitor was discontinued in December 2003.

By April 2004, Mr. Sullivan felt that his overall level of muscle strength had improved and that the amount of muscle cramping he was experiencing had diminished.

However, in May 2004, he developed a right-foot drop and was diagnosed as having a peroneal neuropathy.

In July 2004, Mr. Sullivan experienced a flare-up of a longstanding cervical radiculopathy. He experienced radicular pain and numbness in a C7 distribution. He tells me that he had intermittently experienced similar radicular pain over the past five years.

In September 2004, he developed weakness of the right thumb with loss of extension and abduction strength. At this point in time, he was referred for a neurosurgical consultation.

On October 14, 2004, he underwent surgery which consisted of a C8 foraminotomy. The surgery was a success in that his radicular right upper extremity pain and numbness disappeared. However, weakness in the right thumb persists.

Over the last several months, Mr. Sullivan has also experienced progressive, bilateral lower extremity weakness. At the present time, he reports bilateral distal lower extremity weakness at nighttime. He does not report significant difficulties with muscle cramping. He feels that his voice may have been a little more raspy than usual over the last couple of weeks, but he is not sure of this. He has not experienced any difficulties with chewing, swallowing or breathing.

Mr. Sullivan has undergone neurologic workup by his Maine neurologist, who did recently make a diagnosis of ALS. The workup has included multiple EMG studies with the most recent EMGs being performed in early December 2004. They show normal sensory studies and low motor amplitudes in the bilateral lower extremities and for the right median nerve. Workup also included a lumbosacral spine MRI, December 7, 2004, which showed diffuse degenerative changes, but no spinal stenosis or foramenal stenosis. Cervical spine MRI performed prior to the C8 foraminotomy is reported to show a bony bar at the C7-T1 level on the right compressing the C8 nerve root.

Serum CK was 423 in December 2004. Mr. Sullivan recently had a pulmonary function test, which showed his forced vital capacity was 83 percent of predicted.

Mr. Sullivan was started on Riluzole 50 mg approximately a month ago.

Past Medical History:
1. History of anxiety.
2. History of parasitic diarrheal illness 4 years ago.
3. GERD resulting in laryngeal stridor.
4. Elevated cholesterol.
5. Hypertension.

Family History: There is no known history of neuromuscular disease. At this time, Mr. Sullivan's mother is alive and well at age 83. His father died at age 48 of suicide. There is a positive history of Alzheimer's disease on Mr. Sullivan's father's side of the family. Mr. Sullivan has two children of his own, ages 32 and 29, who are healthy.

Social History: Mr. Sullivan works as a university administrator. He lives with his wife in a two-story home. He does not smoke or drink alcohol.

Review of Systems: A complete review of systems was performed and is negative, except for the positives noted in history of present illness.

Physical Exam: Mr. Sullivan is in no acute distress. General exam is notable for some wasting of the distal lower extremity muscles bilaterally. In addition, there is some atrophy of the

159

right abductor pollicis brevis muscle. There is suggestion of tongue fasciculation, but this is not clear-cut. Cramping was experienced with manual muscle testing of the knee extensors. Vibratory perception is slightly diminished in the toes. Muscle stretch reflexes are 3+ with spread for the bilateral biceps, triceps, brachioradialis. Knee jerks are 3+ bilaterally and ankle jerks 2+. Toes are down going in response to plantar stimulus. Upper extremity coordination is within normal limits. Gait is notable for decreased heel strike on the right. Mr. Sullivan is able to walk on his toes, but not his heels.

Impression and Recommendations: Mr. Sullivan is a 59-year-old gentleman with a one-and-a-half year history of progressive bilateral lower extremity weakness and right upper extremity weakness. On physical exam, he has diffuse hyperreflexia in addition to the muscle weakness mentioned above. Unfortunately, the most likely diagnosis is ALS. I discussed this in detail with Mr. Sullivan and his wife. I did tell them that we would like to repeat his EMG study, order an MRI of the brain, and obtain the following laboratory studies: CBC, sedimentation rate, general chemistry panel, magnesium, calcium and phosphorus levels, serum lead level, 24-hour urine collection for heavy metals, RPR, serum protein electrophoresis, urine assay for Bence-Jones proteins, Hepatitis panel, Lyme titer, ANA and rheumatoid factor.

After that initial visit, I asked Dr. Krivickas to be my ALS specialist. She agreed.

Primary Care Physician - Progress Notes - 01/27/2005

Gary has seen the ALS specialist in Boston. The most likely diagnosis, according to the specialist, is also amyotrophic lateral sclerosis. He is having emotional troubles with depression. He has spent a lot of time sleeping. Much of the time in today's visit is spent counseling and discussing issues related with his diagnosis. He would like to take a positive approach towards things and pursue full activity as long as he can. He does describe that he gets tired easily and some days are better than others.

Primary Care Physician - Progress Notes - 05/26/2005

Gary has had very little to no progression of the disease. Unfortunately, he does have to use a brace on his right leg. Emotionally, he has dealt with this disease extremely well so far. Initially, he was getting depressed, but Gary has retained his sense of humor and is involved in community work, including some local boards.

ALS Specialist - Medical Notes - 08/02/2005

Mr. Sullivan reports that his right-hand strength is stable. He has been wearing his right ankle-foot orthosis (AFO) on a regular basis and feels that he is able to walk quite well without any other assistive device. He does note that he occasionally develops a left-foot drop after walking for a prolonged period of time. Mr. Sullivan has some intermittent left shoulder pain with abduction. He does not report any difficulties with swallowing or chewing. Mr. Sullivan recently enrolled in the Coenzyme Q10 clinical trial.

Physical Exam: On neurologic exam, cranial nerves II through XII are intact. However, there are a few tongue fasciculations, and there is a gravelly quality to the voice. Toes are down going in response to plantar stimulus. We discussed the fact that he may need a left AFO at some point in the near future. His FVC was 78% of predicted sitting and 75% of predicted lying down.

Primary Care Physician - Progress Notes - 08/10/2005

Mr. Sullivan was somewhat reassured by the fact that he has slow progressive ALS as per his specialist's (MGH) interpretation. His spirits appear to be good. I also discussed about hyperlipidemia[15]. He states that he has been trying to put on weight and eating everything in sight. He is determined not to be on statins, as he thinks there may be an association between statins and ALS. His weight is 175 pounds.

ALS Specialist - Medical Notes - 11/01/2005

Gary is now approximately two-and-a-half years since the initial onset of symptom and seems to be progressing slowly. He remains independent with all activities of daily living and is driving without any difficulties. His forced vital capacity is 76% of predicted. His maximum inspiratory and expiratory pressures and 61 and 62% of predicted, respectively.

<u>Physical Exam:</u> He does appear to have a few tongue fasciculations, and there is a gravelly quality to his voice which has not changed over the course of the last year. The right toe is mute and the left toe up going in response to plantar stimulus. Gait appears stable using the right AFO. However, there is a lack of left heel strike.

ALS Specialist - Medical Notes - 12/20/2005

Mr. Sullivan continues to progress slowly. He does note that his leg seems to be fatiguing more easily than it has in the past and he is relying more on his right leg. I did give him a prescription for a left PLS (posterior leaf spring) style AFO which he will have manufactured in Maine.

---

[15] Hyperlipidemia: High lipid (fat) levels in the blood.

ALS Specialist - Medical Notes - 02/14/2006

Mr. Sullivan continues to ambulate with a right PLS AFO and a straight cane held in the right hand. He has been fitted for a left PLS and is expecting to receive this brace in two weeks. He does not report any falls. There are a few tongue fasciculations, and there is a somewhat gravely quality to the voice. His FVC is 75 of predicted both seated and supine.

ALS Specialist - Medical Notes - 04/11/2006

Mr. Sullivan has received a new left PLS-style AFO since our last visit. He is ambulating with bilateral PLS-style AFOs at the present time but is not happy with the new brace on the left foot. He feels that it actually slows him down. Mr. Sullivan also reports some intermittent numbness of the fifth digit of the right hand as well as some intermittent right forearm pain. These symptoms are reminiscent of those he had with an active cervical radiculopathy at the C8 level in the past. Mr. Sullivan reports that his speech is slightly more dysarthric than it has been previously and that he does occasionally bite his tongue. He feels that he has been slightly more depressed over the last several weeks.

This is Mr. Sullivan's last Coenzyme Q10 study visit. He plans to begin taking Coenzyme Q10 outside the study, and I have recommended 1,200 mg per day.

Physical Examination: Mr. Sullivan's weight is 176 lbs. Cranial nerves II through XII are intact with the exception of a few tongue fasciculations and decreased tongue mobility as well as a very mild dysarthria. It does appear that his left leg brace is set in slightly too much dorsiflexion so that it takes too long for the toe to strike. There is also a slight Trendelenburg component to the gait today.

Impressions and Recommendations: I recommended that Mr. Sullivan return to the orthotist who made the left PLS for him and have the brace modified so that it is in 2 to 3 degrees of more plantar flexion. I believe that this will smooth out his gait somewhat. His maximum inspiratory pressure was 55% of predicted and maximum expiratory pressure 78% of predicted. FVC is 69% of predicted seated, 66% supine.

ALS Specialist - Medical Notes - 07/11/2006

Mr. Sullivan reports that he has experienced a slight increase in right-hand weakness and decrease in balance since his last visit. However, he remains quite active with activities outside the home and is independent with all activities of daily living. He reports occasional coughing when drinking liquids but no other swallowing difficulties. He has lost approximately four pounds since his last visit because of a decrease in appetite. He does not report any respiratory symptoms. He does report that he is having a difficult time psychologically adjusting to the use of the cane.

Physical Exam: Cranial nerves II through XII are intact with the exception of mild tongue atrophy, tongue fasciculations, decreased tongue mobility and mild dysarthria.

Impression and Recommendations: Mr. Sullivan is doing remarkably well at the present time. I did suggest that we consider performing a swallowing study some time in the near future if he begins to experience more coughing with thin liquids. FVC is 79% of predicted.

Primary Care Physician - Progress Notes - 08/09/2006

Chief complaint: Follow up of ALS. Mr. Sullivan is describing new and increased difficulty swallowing, problems with speech. Examination of the tongue revealed fasciculations.

As a result of an increasing concern regarding my swallowing and the potential for choking, I was examined by a speech pathologist at MGH in September 2006.

Radiology Report - MGH - 09/07/2006

History: Mr. Sullivan is a 61-year-old male diagnosed with ALS in 2004. He has noted that over the past six months to a year swallowing has become a more conscious task, both with regard to oral manipulation and initiation of the pharyngeal swallow. He also feels that he has had increased saliva in the oral cavity. Over the past year he has lost ten pounds, though he is making every effort to increase caloric intake. He reports that he occasionally is avoiding foods that are difficult to chew and that meal time has increased markedly to greater than 45 minutes. Mr. Sullivan has noticed a change in his speech and voice, specifically changed vocal quality.

Contrast: Patient was administered multiple large sips of ultrathin liquid barium, pudding mixed with barium paste x2 tsp. and cookie coated with barium past. Patient was viewed in the lateral and A-P planes.

Findings: A complete oral peripheral exam and assessment of speech were completed prior to presentation of contrast. Patient was found to have bilateral tongue fasciculations and atrophy, slow and regular AMR's and SMR's, and a weak cough. Patient had low to moderate difficulty with bolus formation and control for all consistencies. Contrast was seen to spill over lateral aspect of the time and not the lateral sulci. There was complete BOT to posterior pharyngeal wall contact. The onset of the swallow was timely, but there was decreased anterior excursion of the larynx during the swallow. Airway closure was noted to be complete with no penetration or aspiration noted with any consistency or bolus size. Pharyngeal contractions were reduced with residue noted along the posterior pharyngeal wall and pyriform sinuses. With head rotation to the left and the right, pharyngeal stripping was markedly improved with patient reducing number of swallows required to clear pharynx (five down to two).

<u>Impressions:</u> Patient presents with a mild oropharyngeal dysphagia secondary to diagnosis of ALS. In the oral stage, he was noted to have decreased manipulation and organization of boluses of all consistencies. In the pharyngeal stripping with resultant residue especially with solids. He benefits significantly from simple positional strategies, rotating head to the left or to the right to help facilitate pharyngeal stripping, and is encouraged to use these positional strategies to reduce pharyngeal residue and minimize risk of aspiration. With regard to speech, Mr. Sullivan has a mild flaccid dysarthria and is judged to be 100-percent intelligible at this time.

<u>Recommendations:</u>
1. Patient should take small single bites of solid foods.
2. Patient and his wife should contact their local Red Cross office to learn the Heimlich maneuver.
3. Patient should utilize head rotation to the left or the right shoulder when swallowing solid foods. This helps to facilitate pharyngeal stripping and minimize residue left in the pharynx after the swallow. The same strategy can be used if he feels that solid foods are sticking in the pharynx, even when the rotation has not been used during the previous swallow.
4. Patient should take small single sips of liquid.

ALS Specialist - Medical Notes - 10/17/2006

Mr. Sullivan did have a video fluoroscopic swallowing examination September 7. It showed trace penetration without aspiration. He did receive some counseling from speech therapy following the study and has been instructed in some compensatory techniques. Mr. Sullivan does express a fear of choking and believes that he has cut down on his oral intake because of this.

Physical Exam: Cranial nerve exam is notable for some mild lower facial weakness. The tongue is slightly atrophic with fasciculations and decreased range of motion. I also note a few fasciculations on the chin. There is mild dysarthria, which has a lower motor neuron quality.

Impression and Recommendations: I did recommend that Mr. Sullivan eat multiple small meals and snacks throughout the day and possibly use a high-calorie supplement to increase his caloric intake. I do not want to see him lose any more weight.

***

2007

ALS Specialist - Medical Notes - 01/16/2007

Mr. Sullivan has not had any falls. He does report some increased difficulty with coordinating his swallowing and with his choking. He has lost 24 pounds since he initially developed symptoms of ALS. Mr. Sullivan does not report any respiratory symptoms at the present time.

Physical Exam: Cranial nerve exam is notable for some mild lower muscle weakness. The tongue is atrophic with fasciculations and decreased range of motion. There is mild dysarthria. There is a slight Trendelenburg component that may be slightly more prominent than it was at his last visit.

Impressions and Recommendations: He remains stable from a functional standpoint.

ALS Specialist - Medical Notes - 04/10/2007

Mr. Sullivan's disease duration is almost 4 years now. He is not currently reporting any respiratory symptoms. He does note that he is finding it increasingly difficult to walk around his house without his AFOs. He is walking approximately ¼ mile as his maximum distance. He continues to drive without difficulty. He notes that his bathroom is handicapped-equipped and has grab bars. He does not have any difficulties with performing activities in the bathroom. Mr. Sullivan does report an increase in hand muscle cramping when doing a lot of typing on the computer. He does not have any other symptoms related to upper extremity weakness. Mr. Sullivan reports that his current weight is 155 pounds. Thus he has lost four additional pounds since his last clinic. He is eating well and does not note any change in his baseline dysphagia. He does occasionally experience throat spasms that make it difficult for him to breathe for up to several minutes.

Primary Care Physician - Progress Notes - 05/09/2007

Gary presents to the office for follow-up on amyotrophic lateral sclerosis. He has had clear progression of his symptoms. His toes are immovable and are curled up. He is having weakness to the point that he has to wear his brace all the time. Previously, at home, he was not wearing his brace. We had a detailed discussion about a Living Will, which he has filled out. We also talked about treating his cholesterol. He would not like his cholesterol treated. He will not take statins because he has the belief that the statins play a role in worsening ALS. End-of-life issues were discussed.

ALS Specialist - Medical Notes - 07/24/2007

Mr. Sullivan reports that he feels fairly stable from a functional standpoint. He has had no falls. He does note that his endurance for ambulation had decreased somewhat. He is able to go a few 100 feet before having to stop and rest. His weight dropped from 160 to 151 pounds but has now increased to 155 pounds. Mr. Sullivan does not report any difficulties with shortness of breath, and he generally sleeps well.

Impression and Recommendations: Mr. Sullivan requested a prescription for a walker. I gave him a prescription for a Rollator-style walker with a seat.

Primary Care Physician - Progress Notes - 09/05/2007

Gary's ALS is showing clear signs of progression. He is having trouble with prolonged periods of eating. He is also starting to use a walker. Gary's wishes are for no prolonged life support. He is more interested in quality of life rather than quantity of life. We briefly talked about a feeding tube. He does not want a tracheotomy when the time comes for the need of a tracheotomy. He and his family are well aware of this.

ALS Specialist - Medical Notes - 10/23/2007

Mr. Sullivan's disease duration is now a little more than four years. He does note that he is slightly more fatigued when ambulating than he has been in the past. Mr. Sullivan reports that he occasionally has a sensation of heavy breathing at night time. However, he reports that his sleep is good and uninterrupted. Pulmonary function tests performed today show an FVC that is 66% of predicted in the seated position and 58% of predicted in the supine position. MIP and MEP are 32% and 50% of predicted respectively. Liver function tests were checked at the last visit and were within normal limits.

Impressions and Recommendations: Because of Mr. Sullivan's declining forced vital capacity and report of "heavy breathing" at night, we have decided to start him on nocturnal BiPAP. This will give him plenty of time to accommodate to the treatment before his respiratory muscle declines further.

Primary Care Physician - Progress Notes - 12/05/2007

Gary is unable to get in and out of his house comfortably. He is going to get a ramp put in. A letter of support for a ramp is dictated today.

Advanced Directives: Gary brings in a copy of advanced directives. He would not like life support or resuscitation under any circumstances.

***

2008

ALS Specialist - Medical Notes - 01/29/2008

Mr. Sullivan currently uses his PLS-style AFOs at all times when ambulating within the home. He has also noticed some increased weakness about the left shoulder, such that he is having difficulty with overhead activities. He is also experiencing some loss of shoulder range of motion and some shoulder pain on the left.

Mr. Sullivan feels his dysarthria may have increased slightly, but he is still communicating very effectively. He reports that he has gained five pounds since his last visit.

Mr. Sullivan has begun using BiPAP nocturnally. He uses it 3-4 hours per night but takes one night off per week. FVC is 66% of predicted in the seated position.

Physical Exam: Mr. Sullivan's left shoulder abduction and external rotations are grade 3+/5. There is a positive impingement sign on the left. There is also mild shoulder subluxation.

Primary Care Physician - Progress Notes - 02/27/2008

Gary would like to try Lithium for ALS. He has spoken to his ALS specialist, who has also looked at some preliminary studies with Lithium. These are animal studies. Gary understands the risk of this approach. His specialist also recommends that it is worth a try; monitoring has been delineated. Start Lithium and check blood work prior to next visit.

My blood workup showed an elevated white cell count.

Primary Care Physician - Progress Notes - 03/19/2008

Gary has started Lithium
Assessment: Some improvement in symptomatology with Lithium. Increase it to 150 mgs. Three times a day.

Primary Care Physician - Progress Notes - 04/11/2008

Follow up of elevated white cell count: Gary had an elevated white count of 17,500. The differential does look as though Gary may have chronic lymphocytic leukemia (CLL). However, his last blood cell count done on February 4, 2005, was essentially unremarkable. Given that he has no anemia, and even if he has CLL, this does not require intervention, especially in Gary who is also suffering from progressive ALS. We discussed this in detail. We decided to repeat a CBC today and, if elevated, go ahead and do flow cytometry for a final diagnosis. I answered questions about whether this could affect his prognosis with ALS, which clearly would be unknown. No lymphadenopathy palpated in the neck, axilla or groin.

Primary Care Physician - Progress Notes - 04/23/2008

Gary's routine blood work done for lithium monitoring showed an elevated white cell count. Flow cytometry shows chronic lymphocytic leukemia. Gary has taken this diagnosis in stride. He is willing to see the hematologist. This appears to be Stage 1. We had a detailed discussion for approximately 30 minutes about its implication and how it would affect ALS.

Primary Care Physician's letter to Hematologist
I am referring Gary Sullivan to you with a diagnosis of chronic lymphocytic leukemia. Gary also has amyotrophic lateral sclerosis, which is gradually progressive and is managed by a Boston specialist. He has no active complaints, and his CLL was diagnosed based on routine CBC.

ALS Specialist - Medical Notes - 05/06/2008

Gary Sullivan's disease duration is almost five years. Unfortunately, Mr. Sullivan was recently diagnosed with CLL. No treatment is being recommended at the current time.

Mr. Sullivan has been taking Lithium for several months now. He recently discontinued taking Coenzyme Q10 when he heard that the clinical trial in which he participated had negative results

Physical Examination: Cranial nerve exam is notable for mild shoulder abduction weakness. Muscle stretch reflexes are 2+ and symmetric throughout the upper extremities and 2+ at the knees. FVC is 62% of predicted.

Primary Care Physician - Progress Notes - 05/28/2008

Gary presents to the office today for an acute visit due to left shoulder pain with raising his arms over his head. He had shoulder X-rays that showed degenerative changes at the AC joint bilaterally. He developed increasing pain in his left shoulder, which radiated down to the elbow and to the wrist. He has numbness and tingling in the first two fingers of the left hand. He has noticed increased weakness in his hands, although it is difficult to assess given his underlying ALS. He has increased pain at night. He is not able to get comfortable lying down and is only sleeping for 1-2 hours at a time which is interfering with his daily living. He states that his symptoms are very similar to cervical radiculopathy, which he had operated on four years ago.

Left shoulder: no tenderness, no swelling. Range of motion is mildly limited at the extremes of motion, most notably in external rotation.

<u>Assessment & Plan:</u> Shoulder and arm pain - patient would not be interested in pursuing surgery at this time and systemic steroids would not be an ideal long-term treatment option due to the risk of muscle weakness and worsening of ALS symptoms. Will try pain medication for the next 3-5 days and then pursue MRI of neck and shoulder if symptoms are not improved.

ALS Specialist - Medical Notes - 07/29/2008

Mr. Sullivan discontinued taking Lithium approximately two months ago because he felt that it increased his weakness and was causing him to develop a tremor. He notes that his fatigue level has decreased since discontinuing the Lithium. Mr. Sullivan had been experiencing some shoulder pain over the course of the last several months. He had an MRI study, which apparently showed some rotator cuff tendinitis. The pain has subsided significantly, and he is no longer taking any pain medication for it. He has discontinued using BiPAP at night. He had been using it for approximately three hours per night but states that he feels just as good without it.

Mr. Sullivan continues to ambulate using bilateral PLS-style ankle foot orthoses and has a new rolling straight cane. He does report that he is unable to get off the floor without assistance and that he believes he is experiencing a slight increase in weakness in the arms and legs. He continues to drive independently without any adaptations or difficulties.

<u>Physical Examination:</u> Cranial nerve exam is notable for mild lower facial muscle weakness with mild to moderate dysarthria and difficulty pocketing air in the cheeks. There is some tongue atrophy and fasciculation. Neck extensor strength is 5/5, whereas neck flexor strength is 4/5. In the upper extremities, shoulder abduction is 4/5, biceps and triceps 4+/5 and distal strength 5/5. In the lower extremities, hip flexion is 4+/5, knee extension and flexion is 4+/5, ankle dorsiflexion is 2/5 and plantar flexion is 3/5. Muscle stretch reflexes are 2+ and symmetric throughout the upper extremities and at the knees, absent at the ankles.

<u>Impressions and Recommendations:</u> As long as his FVC remains above 50% of predicted and he is asymptomatic, I will not push him to resume using BiPAP machine. FVC is 68%

ALS Specialist - Medical Notes - 10/21/2008

Since Mr. Sullivan's last visit, he feels that he is gradually having increased leg weakness. He mainly notices this on tasks such as difficulty getting off the ground. He also feels that he may have increased arm weakness as well. He will occasionally need to help support the right arm with the left. He does note occasional problems with choking on his own saliva, with the most recent episode being last week.   FVC = 67%

ALS Specialist - Medical Notes - 01/27/2009

<u>History of Present Illness:</u> Since his last visit, Mr. Sullivan has noted a significant increase in upper extremity weakness, particularly on the right. He is having difficulty taking plates off shelves and holding a cup of tea with his right hand without spilling it. He also notes some slight increase in overall fatigue.

He continues to ambulate with bilateral PLS-style ankle-foot orthoses and a rolling cane and is doing quite well. He reports that he was able to Christmas shop for six hours continually without excessive fatigue.

Mr. Sullivan had used BiPAP in the past but has discontinued it because he does not feel he needs it. His FVC has been fairly stable at approximately 67% of predicted.

Mr. Sullivan has mild dysarthria, but it does not seem to have changed significantly since I last saw him.

Mr. Sullivan does have one new complaint today. Approximately five minutes after he eats a meal, he experiences a rush of frothy liquid into his mouth. This was discussed with our speech pathologist, and we believe that it may be a form of gastroesophageal reflux. I have recommended that he get a referral to a gastroenterologist and possibly have the issue looked at endoscopically.

Mr. Sullivan is otherwise medically stable. He is followed by Hematology for his chronic lymphocytic leukemia.

<u>Physical Examination</u>: Cranial nerve exam is notable for some mild lower facial muscle weakness with mild dysarthria and difficulty pocketing air in the cheeks. There is some tongue atrophy and fasciculations. Neck flexor and extensor strength are 4 out of 5. In the upper extremities, shoulder abduction is 3/5 on the right and 4 out of 5 on the left. Biceps and triceps are both 4/5. Distal upper extremity strength is a grade 3 out of 5 on the right and 3/5 on the left. In the lower extremities, hip flexion, knee extension and knee flexion are all 4/5. Muscle stretch reflexes are two and symmetric throughout the upper extremities and at the knees. Mr. Sullivan is wearing his bilateral AFOs. He has not had any difficulty with skin issues. His gait was observed using his rolling walker and appeared quite stable.

Impressions and Recommendations: I have given Mr. Sullivan a referral to occupational therapy for an assessment of his ADLs and recommendation of some adaptive devices such as utensils with build-up handles and a zipper pull. I also recommended that he consult a gastroenterologist about his reflux problem. We will check a forced vital capacity, weight, and his liver function tests before he leaves clinic today. Mr. Sullivan will follow up with me again in three months. The majority of our half-hour visit was spent in counseling and coordination of care. FVC is 69% predicted.

Speech Pathologist - Notes - 01/27/2009

Speech Severity: Speech is consistently impaired. Affected are rate, articulation and resonance. Remains easily understood.

Swallowing Severity: Mealtime has significantly increased and smaller bite sizes are necessary.

Mr. Sullivan was seen for follow-up in the ALS/ Neuromuscular Clinic. He reports little change in speech or swallow function since our last meeting in July 2007. He reports that he has been able to maintain his weight, supplementing his diet with foods such as donuts, cakes, and muffins. Patient reports that it typically takes 45 minutes to complete a meal, following previous recommendations of smaller bites of solid food and taking small single sips of liquid. He currently chews primarily on the right side of his mouth. Patient complained that dairy products are causing him to experience a rush of a white, frothy, thick, mucous-like consistency in his mouth. Clinician believes this is related to his GERD, and suggests he consult his gastroenterologist. He continues with a mild flaccid dysarthria and is judged to be 100% intelligible. He reports that his voice gets "tired" by the end of the day and it is more difficult to produce speech. Today's oral/peripheral exam revealed mildly weak tongue protrusion and moderately weak lateralization. Tongue with scalloping along left side and back of right tongue.

Recommendations:

1. *Treament*: None at this time
2. *Recommended referrals:* Gastroenterologist
3. *Diet Consistency recommendations*: Continue taking smaller bites of solid food. Avoid small textured foods such as nuts, shredded coconut, sprinkles, etc.

References

1. All medical terms cited are from MedicineNet.com which is an online, healthcare media publishing company, owned and operated by WebMD and part of the WebMD Network.

I Prefer to Laugh

CHAPTER 17

ALS~MAINE COLLABORATIVE

The early struggles of my childhood and my academic challenges have had an impact on how I've approached life. I learned early on that if I allowed my limitations to dictate my life, I would become incapable of achievement. My challenge was to find a way to accomplish tasks using the tools that were available to me.

I have learned that life is not about what you cannot do – but what you can do.

When facing challenges the key to success is to accept *similar ends* by using the *means* available.

I have known since December 8, 2004, that I will never win my battle with Lou Gehrig's disease, so I have chosen to do what I am capable of and that is to fight my illness on my terms.

A year after being diagnosed, I joined the board of directors of the ALS Association Northern New England Chapter (ALSANNE). I knew when I signed on that I would not be able to complete the two-year-term, but I thought I could at least give 12 to 18 months toward that effort.

No one was more surprised than I when I completed the full term in February 2008.

In the summer of that year, a dear friend, Ted Hissong, through his Hissong Group, sponsored the first annual *Gary Sullivan ALS Golf Tournament.* His vice-president, Joan Tishkevich, chaired the tournament. That first tournament raised more than $25,000 for the fight to defeat ALS.

That event got my creative juices flowing, and the concept of the *ALS~Maine Collaborative* was formed.

The state of Maine, with its vast geographic area and dispersed population, presents serious challenges to organizations and services in their efforts to serve the state's ALS population. As a result, Maine's people with ALS (pALS) have fewer services available to them than their counterparts in the rest of New England.

So what could be done to address Maine's challenges in dealing with Lou Gehrig's disease?

As I have done throughout my life, I looked for individuals with whom I could partner to answer that question.

That's where Orm Irish and Lee Urban came in.

Orm and I served together on the ALSANNE Board of Directors and became good friends. Orm lost his wife to ALS several years ago, and he has been a strong advocate for establishing an ALS clinic in Maine.

I first met Lee while working on an ALS event with the Portland Sea Dogs, a Double-A minor league affiliate of the Boston Red Sox. Lee's wife had just been diagnosed with ALS. I am sad to say that she passed away in the spring of 2009.

Lee shared Orm's and my passion to attack ALS on as many fronts as possible.

The ALS~Maine Collaborative was incorporated on December 30, 2008.

It is the mission of the ALS~Maine Collaborative to establish a statewide presence specific to addressing Amyotrophic Lateral Sclerosis (ALS) in Maine and to help coordinate the services available to persons with ALS, their caregivers, and the groups and organizations that support them by eliminating duplication of care and through the promotion of collaboration and education.

The goal of the Collaborative is to:

- Advocate for pALS and their caregivers;
- Educate the general population about ALS;
- Expand ALS awareness throughout Maine's medical community in general and in its neurological practices in particular;
- Provide an education/service center to serve as a resource to which pALS may be referred; and
- Establish an ALS-specific clinic in Maine.

Maine's top ALS service providers that have joined the Collaborative are:

- E-Hope
- Veterans Affairs Medical Center at Togus
- Maine Hospice Council
- Muscular Dystrophy Association (MDA)
- ALS Association – Northern New England Chapter (ALSANNE)

Because of the combined efforts of these organizations, work is now underway to improve the quality of life for Maine's pALS.

For more information on the ALS~Maine Collaborative go to its website at www.alsmaine.org.

3287595

Made in the USA